FORERUNNERS: IDEAS FIRST FROM THE UNIVERSITY OF
MINNESOTA PRESS

Original e-works to spark new scholarship

FORERUNNERS: IDEAS FIRST is a thought-in-process series of break-through digital works. Written between fresh ideas and finished books, Forerunners draws on scholarly work initiated in notable blogs, social media, conference plenaries, journal articles, and the synergy of academic exchange. This is gray literature publishing: where intense thinking, change, and speculation take place in scholarship.

la paperson
A Third University Is Possible

Akira Mizuta Lippit
Cinema without Reflection: Jacques Derrida's Echopoiesis and Narcissism Adrift

P. David Marshall
The Celebrity Persona Pandemic

Reinhold Martin
Mediators: Aesthetics, Politics, and the City

Shannon Mattern
Deep Mapping the Media City

Kelly Oliver
Carceral Humanitarianism: Logics of Refugee Detention

Davide Panagia
Ten Theses for an Aesthetics of Politics

Jussi Parikka
The Anthrobscene

Chuck Rybak
UW Struggle: When a State Attacks Its University

Steven Shaviro
No Speed Limit: Three Essays on Accelerationism

Sharon Sliwinski
Mandela's Dark Years: A Political Theory of Dreaming

Aspirational Fascism

Aspirational Fascism
The Struggle for Multifaceted
Democracy under Trumpism

William E. Connolly

University of Minnesota Press

MINNEAPOLIS

Portions of "The Rhetorical Strategies of Hitler and Trump" were previously published in "Trump, the Working Class, and Fascist Rhetoric," *theory & event* 20, no. 1 Supplement (January 2017): 23–37.

Published by the University of Minnesota Press, 2017
111 Third Avenue South, Suite 290
Minneapolis, MN 55401–2520
http://www.upress.umn.edu

The University of Minnesota is an equal-opportunity educator and employer.

Fascism, *OED*

1

a. Usu. with capital initial. A nationalist political movement that controlled the government of Italy from 1922
to 1943 under the leadership of Benito Mussolini (1883–
1945); the principles or ideology of the *fascisti* (**fascista
n. 1a**). See also **fascist *n.* 1a**, **Fascismo *n.***, and cf. sense
1b. Now *hist.*

The movement grew out of the nationalist *fasci* which
became prominent at the end of the First World War . . . ,
esp. with the formation of the militantly anti-communist
and anti-socialist *Fasci di Combattimento* by Mussolini
in 1919. After the formation of a coherently organized
Fascist party in 1921, Mussolini became prime minister
in 1922, leading to the eventual establishment of a totali-
tarian Fascist state.

1921 *Syracuse* (N.Y.) *Daily Herald* 1 Feb. 2/3 No doubt fascism is a transitory phenomenon.

1921 *Manch. Guardian* 20 May 8/4 Socialists desire to co-
operate, but cannot forgive Signor Giolitti for his toler-
ation towards Fascism.

1922 *Q. Rev.* Jan. 148 A section of the Press . . . now veered
completely round to the cause of Fascism. The Fascist
terror increased in intensity. . . .

1933 *Times* 2 Nov. 13/2 Fascism, as Signor Mussolini has
written . . . did not spring from any pre-established plan. It
began in action against Communists and Socialists.

1948 *Bks. Abroad* 22 133 We have given asylum to the perse-
cuted of Europe, to the refugees from Nazism and Fascism.

2009 *Art Q.* Summer 80/1 Futurism expressed the dynamism and energy of life in the early 20th century, glori-
fying war and the machine age and supporting the rise
of Fascism.

b. *gen.* An authoritarian and nationalistic system of government and social organization which emerged after
the end of the First World War in 1918, and became a
prominent force in European politics during the 1920s
and 1930s, most notably in Italy and Germany; (later
also) an extreme right-wing political ideology based on
the principles underlying this system. Freq. with capital
initial. Cf. fascist *n.* **1b.**

Fascism originated in Italy as an anti-communist and
nationalist movement (see sense **1a**). In the 1920s and,
particularly, the 1930s, political parties and groups were
founded on the Italian model in numerous countries, including Britain, Brazil, France, Hungary, Romania, Spain,
and above all Germany (see, e.g., Falange *n.*, Iron Guard
n. at iron *adj.* Special uses 2, Nazism *n.*). These parties
typically opposed socialism and liberalism (as well as
communism) and advocated ultranationalistic policies,
usually espousing ethnocentric ideas of racial superiority,
esp. anti-Semitism. Where such parties came to power, as
in Italy and Germany, they characteristically formed to-
talitarian dictatorships, giving special status to a charismatic leader (cf. Duce *n.*, Führer *n.*) and often pursuing
an aggressively militaristic foreign policy. After the defeat
of Nazi Germany and Fascist Italy in the Second World
War (1939–45), Fascism ceased to be a significant political force, although subsequently (chiefly from the 1970s)
a number of extreme right-wing nationalist parties have
been founded in Europe and elsewhere on similar principles (cf. neo-fascism *n.*, neo-Nazism *n.*).

1923 *Contemp. Rev.* Nov. 557 Fascism in Germany will never be more than one of several factors.

1934 tr. K. Heiden *National Socialism* xvii. 354 The electoral victories all over Europe with which the Labour Parties have replied to German Fascism.

1936 *Discovery* Dec. 378/1, I have strongly criticised modern education and the methods of handling youth generally as inculcating excessive respect for authority and thereby conducing to the growth of Fascism.

1947 S. Cloete *Third Way* v. 55 There is no middle course to be steered between fascism and communism.

1972 A. J. P. Taylor *Let.* 30 Oct. in *Lett. to Eva* (1991) 96 What will future historians say? Will they understand, as we do, that Fascism had to be destroyed?

2013 *Exmouth Jrnl.* (Nexis) 14 Mar. The EU seems hell bent on creating exactly those same social conditions . . . that led to the rise of fascism in Italy, Germany and Spain and caused the Second World War.

2. In extended use *(depreciative)*.

a. Any form of behaviour perceived as autocratic, intolerant, or oppressive; *esp.* the advocacy of a particular viewpoint or practice in a manner that seeks to enforce conformity. Cf. fascist *n.* **2a.**

1939 D. Thomas *Let.* July (1987) 389, I think that to fight, for instance, the fascism of bad ideas by uniforming & regimenting good ones will be found, eventually, to be bad tactics.

1968 *N.Y. Mag.* 11 Nov. 55/3 The Living Theatre treats us to a threefold fascism. The fascism of mercilessly inflicted vulgarity and boredom, the fascism of global intolerance, and the fascism of profound disrespect for human creativity and art.

1973 *Times* 13 Oct. 14 There is a fundamental fascism of the left which is the real problem in the universities: they are theologically right, as they believe, and you are so wrong that you should even be denied the freedom to speak.

1997 *Guardian* 21 June 16/4 One critic . . . found himself barred from Thursday's press review after the curator accused him of "fascism and pornography."

2007 www.adamsmith.org/blog (Nexis) 28 Apr. When modern filtration can make the air even cleaner than it was before anyone lit up, an outright ban is just fascism—an attempt by one group to impose its own choice of lifestyle on another.

b. With modifying word, specifying the particular aspect of life or sphere of activity concerned. Cf. fascist *n.* **2b.**

body, eco-, health fascism: see the first element.

1958 A. Ellis *Sex without Guilt* xiv. 168 Sex fascism is a major subheading under what I call intellectual fascism—which I find . . . to be perhaps the most pandemic and virulent psychosocial disease of our times.

1970 *Rags* Oct. (front cover), Fashion fascism—politics of midi.

1974 B. Hoddeson *Porn People* vii. 121/1 You get a sort of monosexual fascism that takes place, that says, "this is how you'll ball."

1992 *Independent* 15 July 20/8 Now councils introducing restraint are accused of "green fascism."

2013 *Sun* (Nexis) 21 Feb. (Scotl. ed.) 15 [His] obsession with food fascism reached new heights this week with a demand that the entire . . . Staples Centre in Los Angeles should be cleared of all meat products before he takes the stage.

Contents

Preface: Apples and Oranges

IT WAS THE MIDDLE OF JULY 2016. Hillary Clinton was riding high, and the media had not yet entirely overcome the drive to reduce the campaign of Donald Trump to a humorous series of mix-ups, historical mistakes, tweet misspellings, and name callings. My sister, my partner, and I stopped at a café in the northwestern part of the lower peninsula of Michigan; we had been vacationing there with a large family entourage on one of those gorgeous lakes where the white sand runs thick, the water is clear, and the sunsets are stunning. The glacier melt ten thousand years ago had been good to this part of the world, forming the Great Lakes and distributing innumerable small pearls of blue framed by tall pine trees.

It is also an area where white flight from southern Michigan is pronounced and Republicans are regularly favored in elections up and down the ticket. Politics was not on our minds that day as my two companions and I settled in to enjoy the pie the Cherry Hut had made famous in the region. I sipped a cup of coffee and begged a small bite now and then. We were recovering from a day of kayaking and rollicking in the water with kids of varying ages.

Five working-class vacationers walked into that café, sitting a table away from us. The alpha male wore a severe look, a baseball cap, and an aggressive T-shirt; he spoke in short, definitive phrases. I grew up as a working-class boy in an urban, southern part of that state speckled with such types. Some of us made fun of that definitive demeanor behind their backs from time to time, though we also had a sense of the pain and authoritarian discipline that contributed to their way of being. We had dads, uncles, barbers, coaches, and neighbors. We did not yet know that to mimic can also be to simulate . . .

A soft-spoken man, a woman cued in to her (probable) dominant husband, and another woman a bit older and mild in demeanor completed the table. For fifteen minutes the alpha male explained in no-nonsense terms why it was absolutely necessary to defeat Hillary Clinton and elect Donald Trump. The very way of life they prized was at stake. Race was never mentioned in that speech, though the flight of good jobs, the threat posed by immigration, the need for a Wall, the problems with free trade, and the conceits of liberal elites on the two coasts all made appearances in a series of short, jolting phrase jabs. Each phrase was thrown as a punch.

There was no disagreeing with this guy at that table; two of his three partners showed little desire to do so as they ate hamburgers together. The third woman tried to dissent mildly from time to time. She would say, "I hear what you are saying and I have no truck with Hillary, but doesn't Trump scare you a little sometimes?" "No," the man would blurt, "he is exactly what this country needs today!" The two others would nod in concurrence and she would slouch back in a repose lodged somewhere between passive concurrence and silent dissent. The issue, it appeared, was not large enough to test a friendship. Besides, peeking just below that alpha-male bravado were vulnerabilities that doubled the hesitancy his companions showed in dissenting from him. An aggressive, domineering, vulnerable man.

As we left the joint, the three of us shuddered and laughed together, making fun of ourselves for eavesdropping so blatantly and reviewing some questions we would have loved to pose had it been permissible to barge into the conversation. My sister was in a wheelchair and none of us was in the mood for a probable firestorm had we tried to do so. Indeed, I don't recall that well the accent, tone, and demeanor I displayed in southern Michigan, under the influence of a Midwestern atmosphere. So the task would not have been easy.

One of us said, laughing, that she would have asked, "Do you have any idea how misogynistic you and Trump are?" I said, responding with something between feigned and real nervousness,

"Don't do that, I am too old to get into a fight with a husky cracker." I announced that I would ask, "What did you guys think of Bernie Sanders? He did win the Democratic primary in Michigan." I knew the question would sound political sciency; I felt confident the alpha male would have written Sanders off, but I suspected that three or four of the others, had they secured an opportunity to speak, might have expressed an affinity to Sanders. One of my Cherry Hut partners was less confident about them, too. Who knows?

I walked out of that café even more convinced than when I had entered that Donald Trump had a very decent chance of winning the 2016 election. At that point the polls said that Clinton had a steady lead. I did not "predict" he would win, thinking predictions are a poor way to engage in political life. But I did write posts on the blog *The Contemporary Condition* focusing on the dangers of Trump and insisting that a favorable "demographics" was insufficient to defeat him. I found Hillary Clinton to be a very capable debater who nonetheless was unable to make close contact with members of the white working class, even though many of the latter had listened to Barack Obama and Bernie Sanders. Several of my friends in political science pooh-poohed my fears about the election, writing them off as the anxieties of a political theorist who did not really understand how polling works. Even on Tuesday night of the election, one hour before the vote tally began to pour in, I received an e-mail from a friend designed to be reassuring. "I have consulted with a red hot pollster in our department," he said, "and there is no path of victory for Donald Trump." During periods of high anxiety, election polls can become dicey. They tend to slide under a rise in atmospheric pressure.

My research for the last several years has focused on the planetary dynamics of the Anthropocene: how denialism is only one of the problems to address in this domain; how those regions of the world that have generated the fewest CO_2 emissions are also those that typically receive the earliest effects of severe drought, ocean rising, ocean acidification, and extreme storms; how a revolution in the

earth sciences has overturned the old story of planetary gradual-
ism with respect to the intersecting processes of species evolution,
the ocean conveyor system, climate change, and glacier flows; how
the study of a variety of synergies between capitalist emissions and
self-organizing planetary systems of several sorts is thus critical
today; how the "evangelical/capitalist resonance machine" in the
United States promotes highly destructive outlooks and policies in
this domain as it also attracts a section of the white working class;
how the humanities and human sciences in the academy remain too
captured by practices of "cultural internalism" and "sociocentrism"
that inhibit them from going beyond a rejection of climate denialism to address the robust effects of planetary systems on postcolo-
nial life, race, class, territorial walls, and Euro-American anxieties.

Attention to the contemporary fragility of things also encouraged
me to think a bit about what I call aspirational fascism. A 2011 post in
The Contemporary Condition by that title suggested that there was a
gathering storm in the United States that could either be overcome or
acquire more momentum. This new type of fascist aspiration, it was
suggested, would seek to retain party competition while pursuing
legal and illegal means to erode voter turnout of African Americans,
the poor, and other minorities. It would incite members of the white
working class, which had been ignored in recent years, with a series
of false promises; it would push devotees of Islamic faiths into the
forefront of groups to hate; it would place the media under tremen-
dous pressure; it would incite vigilante groups and practice thin deniability about doing so; and it would define the United States as a
"garrison state" while ratcheting up its military bellicosity.[1]

1. See "Aspirational Fascism," *The Contemporary Condition* (blog),
September 2011, http://contemporarycondition.blogspot.de/2011/09
/aspirational-fascism.html. For an earlier post exploring why the radical
Right identifies fascism with any large state and disconnects it from the failures and crises generated by an unregulated market economy, see Connolly,
"What Was Fascism?," *The Contemporary Condition* (blog), June 2010,
http://contemporarycondition.blogspot.com/2010/06/what-was-fascism
.html.

So the Trump phenomenon excited my concern. When we were instructed in August 2016 at Johns Hopkins to announce titles for our spring courses, I announced a graduate seminar called What Was/Is Fascism? The Trump phenomenon, it was clear, would persist as festering drives whether Trump won or lost the election. Campaign chants of "Lock her up!" showed the kind of atmosphere we would encounter even if Clinton were to win.

The seminar, taught in spring 2017, explored some of the varieties, uncertainties, and dangers attached to fascist movements. To concentrate our attention, we focused most on possible synergies between the early stages of the Hitler movement in Germany and the dynamics of the Trump movement in the United States over the last couple of years, as the latter movement has morphed out of the evangelical/capitalist machine that had been in place in the United States for more than forty years.

This brief, preliminary study, which grew out of that seminar, has been written in haste. It is also incomplete. Its justification is that haste might be a good idea now, encouraging us to come to terms with a new period of uncertainty when it is still replete with open possibilities. To wait until things are settled may be to wait too long, though that, too, is uncertain at the moment (July 2017). Yes, a comparison of Trump to Berlusconi or Mussolini could have been valuable. Yes, a comparison to Marine Le Pen would be pertinent. Yes, it is next to impossible that the Trump regime will take the course followed by Hitler from the middle 1930s until the end of World War II, though the danger of a nuclear winter ushered in by an impulsive president with fascist dispositions is nothing to sneeze at.

The comparisons pursued in this study do feel like comparing apples to oranges. But those types of comparisons sometimes bring out salient affinities across differences. Apples are reddish; they emit a bitter/sweet taste; they are typically grown in northern temperate zones. And the ones widely available to consumers today are larger and less potent in healthy ingredients than the pungent ones available in an earlier period. A comparative history of apples is pertinent, and it fits readily into regular practices of comparison in the human sciences.

Oranges are orange, with a more intense orangeness dyed into them today. When you peel one, you find slices that can be eaten one at a time, as juice sometimes runs down your hand and onto your cuff. Oranges provide good nourishment for people with diabetes because of their health benefits and the way the sugar content is absorbed by the body slowly as the metabolic process proceeds. Apples are just okay in that regard, and plums, bananas, peaches, and grapes are worse.

To compare apples and oranges is to highlight differences across a series of partial affinities: both are fruit, are edible, grow on trees, and are today raised through intensive farming. If we were to compare both to tomatoes, the differences would be sharper. But even those comparisons do not reach the point of exploring heterogeneous connections across differences.

I start with the caveat about apples and oranges not only because I have heard it as a phrase of reproach when attending conference talks. A political science teacher I revered as an undergraduate at the Flint University of Michigan used that phrase to criticize me gently for my attempt to compare the social philosophies of John Stuart Mill and Herbert Marcuse in a senior honors paper. He gave me a high grade, but surely only as a concession to decent work I had previously done. "But Professor Bradley," I wanted to say, "this is the kind of comparison needed." So my ears perk up when I hear the phrase today. It makes me think, too, of the kind of work that downplays the importance of heterogeneous injections and connections in the world: the injection of the Neanderthal into *Homo sapiens*; the injection of loose DNA into one-celled organisms to create a nucleated cell, the basis of future evolution; the bumpy process of symbiogenesis between algae and fungi out of which lichens emerged. Now we are talking.

What if the Mill tradition, which plays up preference, happiness, and virtual representation in democratic politics, today allowed elements from a Marcuse tradition to infect it with close attention to the politics of affective contagion—that is, to attend to issues festering in Mill that did not sit comfortably with some of his categories? What, too, if Marcuse had allowed Mill to challenge his ideal of a rational, collective society—one he projected as the alternative to Nazism even before the latter had consolidated power? What if the coldness of classical liberalism and individualism, which Marcuse discerned so sharply, fosters one temptation for many to support fascism during a crisis and critical imaginaries of rational collectivity can be dragged in that direction too?

Heterogeneous connections. Nazism was a toxic infection inserted into Weimar democracy during a period of crisis. Black rot infecting apple trees. The injection of multifaceted pluralism into democracy, on the other hand, is noble in itself and provides a vaccination needed to help insulate democracy from drives to a hostile, fascist takeover. But that conjunction, too, can backfire without a second injection. The injection of strong jolts of egalitarianism into democratic pluralism could clinch the deal, though many pluralists have yet to be convinced in their bones of the critical importance of such injections. We have jumped beyond comparisons between apples and oranges to a world of heterogeneous connections and distinctive assemblages.

But why not call the complex to be examined in America today populism? Populism is often defined as rule in the name of a unified people; it expresses a rebellion of the "masses" against an elite or establishment. There are affinities here. But I don't think the designation quite fits what is happening today. First, some contemporary Left populists, such as Cornel West, Bernie Sanders, and Elizabeth Warren, pursue militant activism. But they do not enact the Big Lie Scenario, initiate destructive rumors against opponents, or collude with hostile foreign powers in electoral campaigns, nor do they pursue antipluralism, militarism, hypernationalism, white triumphalism, close state alliances with private corporate power, corruption of intelligence agencies, or tenacious attempts to curtail minority voting. They may also appreciate the need to fold an affective dimension into multifaceted democracy in ways that few "antipopulists" do. I think it is essential, then, to inject a few populist elements into pluralist, egalitarian democracy. I thus call the current movement crystallized by Trump aspirational fascism to underline the dangers to democracy it poses and to encourage supporters of democracy to inject distinctive modes of affective communication, agitation, and activism into democracy.[2] Antipopulism too easily becomes equated with curtailing multifaceted democracy.

As the time neared to organize this seminar, I came more to think of it as a genealogy of fascism. By the time the course had started, Donald Trump had entered the White House, or rather Mar-a-Lago. Melania Trump was squinting from time to time, as she was paraded up and down hotel and airplane staircases in spike heels. That was enough for marchers in the incredible woman's march in November 2016 to carry prescient signs saying "Free Melania." They were early genealogists of the Donald–Melania relationship.

A genealogy of aspirational fascism could focus, first, on aspects of past events that allow us to dramatize elements in the present that might otherwise slide below close attention. It might also identify subterranean strains that did not become consolidated in the past because others did. Such unconsolidated trends sometimes expose real uncertainties simmering in life; they may thus help us to discern how the future before us opens upon a horizon replete with strains of real uncertainty. A genealogy might

2. For a thoughtful study that seems to equate Trump with populism, see Jan-Werner Muller, *What Is Populism?* (Philadelphia: University of Pennsylvania Press, 2016). For a classic study that, while simmering with insights, lumps all mass movements together in ways that trouble me, see Eric Hoffer, *The True Believer: Thoughts on the Nature of Mass Movements* (New York: Harper, 1951).

additionally encourage us to rethink a series of political ideals that continue to contend for hegemony today. Supporters of those contending ideals were not adequately prepared for the advent of fascism when it arose the first time, even though communists and social democrats did try valiantly to fend it off.

To the extent you present interpretations of the past that insert necessity deeply into it, to that extent, you degrade both the political dimension of cultural life and the element of creativity in politics. To bring out the latter elements does decrease the putative power of explanation, but it does not eliminate that power. Studies studded with words and phrases like precisely, exactly, methodological rigor, and sharp definition—as they also reformulate the work of opponents to catch them in "performative contradictions"—are studies apt to resist the genealogical mode. It is too messy, incomplete, and uncertain in its prognostications for their tastes. They often, too, bypass exploration of how affective communication works through bodily disciplines and rhetorical practices, making people like me worry that they have not grasped adequately either the potential power of fascism or the indispensable role of affective communication of a different sort in multifaceted democracy. They may demand either that the world itself be partitioned into sharp distinctions without pregnant zones of indiscernibility, friction, litter, effervescence, and noise or that "we" must act as if it does so to conform to the necessary dictates of epistemology. They may give "priority" to epistemology and method while genealogists think that those imperatives tacitly convey problematic ontologies of being in a rocky world. They like words such as analysis, represent, method, and explain, while we add to the list genealogy, injection, expression, uncertainty, creativity, and heterogeneous crossings. We practice a minor tradition in the human sciences.

A genealogy also attends to relational bodily practices as it explores shifting modes of affective communication. For both democracy and fascism require affective flows of communication, and the former also mixes them into refined processes of reflection and communication. To ignore the vexed relations between bodily disciplines and selective modes of affective contagion is both to diminish your grasp of fascist movements and to miss a dimension operative in different ways in a culture of multifaceted democracy. That is another reason antipopulism does not capture the agenda of inquiry adopted here.

This study is divided into three chapters. The first focuses on a comparison between the rhetorical strategies of Adolf Hitler in the early going in Germany and the rhetorical style and political ambitions of Donald Trump. Apples and oranges. It takes seriously Hitler's charge in *Mein Kampf* that members of the "professoriate" and "intelligentsia" do not appreciate profoundly enough the power of public speeches to infect and move a large populace primed to listen by historical shocks, resentments, grievances, and embodied dispositions. It is clear that Trump agrees with Hitler on this point—though he does deny reading the book by Hitler Ivana Trump said had been sitting on his bed stand for a time. A study of his distinctive rhetorical style and bodily demeanor on the stump may thus be pertinent. The role of the Big Lie Scenario comes in for inspection in that chapter.

The second chapter, after engaging Tim Mason's account of the working class in Nazi Germany and Freud's canonical study of the pull of narcissistic leaders, drills down to explore comparisons between the bodily practices and demeanor of the *Freikorps* during the early stages of the Nazi movement and the practices and demeanor of many on the cutting edge of Trumpian enthusiasm today. Along the way, it explores possible connections between particular modes of bodily discipline and susceptibility to specific forms of affective communication, that is, to modes of contagion within and below linguistic practice conveyed through gesture, posture, facial expression, distinctive rhythms of expression, hand movements, tones of phrasing, jaw settings, habits of eye contact, and styles of walking. I wish we had a video of the phrase punches thrown at the Cherry Hut that day. They jostled the nervous system.

Freud is enlisted to start that exploration. But both Hitler, the inspired Nazi speaker, and Klaus Theweleit, the brilliant explorer of how the "body armor" of leading Nazis was forged in the early period of that movement, prove helpful. The 1950 book *The Authoritarian Personality,* authored in part by Jewish refugees to the United States who were concerned about emerging trends here, is then put into conversation with those two engagements. Possible resonances between the existential resentments and bodily disciplines of "armored males" in pre-Nazi Germany and many alpha males relaying messages from Trump to sections of the white working class in the United States today come up for review.

The third chapter takes off from those explorations to argue that multifaceted pluralism, joined to both open democratic elections and strong egalitarian drives, constitutes a superb ideal in itself and the best available antidote to aspirational fascism today. That chapter begins with an appreciation of the ways both Franz Neumann and Hannah Arendt showed how Nazism broke down spontaneous pluralism during its early phase in power. Then it pursues the terms of a multidimensional practice of pluralism already operative to varying degrees in several quarters today. Some theories of pluralism may be insufficient to today, however. Pluralism needs to include several facets, some of which are now in play and others of which need to receive more power and legitimation. Most critically, a cultural ethos of egalitarianism with respect to income, job security, education prospects, retirement opportunities, and cultural dignity must be injected deeply into democratic pluralism if it is both to thrive and to provide the most effective antidote against a hostile fascist takeover.

At a few points in this study, grievances of the white working and lower middle classes are highlighted. How does a set of racist priorities, bodily practices, authoritarian tendencies, selective receptivity to rhetorical influence, vexed relations to military and corporate heroes, and the "feminization" of presumptive care for outsiders become tempting to some within this variegated constituency? Are there affinities between such temptations now and those in play during the early phase of the Nazi movement? Are there ways that neoliberalism and the pluralizing Left—opposed to one another in fundamental ways—have also combined across these differences to catch this constituency in a bind? These issues, to me, are critical.

There are tensions and uncertainties in my thinking about these issues. I have concluded both that fascism shows how other classical models of collectivism can be dangerous and that the coolness of liberal models of deliberation and the cruelty of neoliberal ruthlessness periodically backfire at moments of crisis in ways that can incite counterdrives to fascism. So I place my bet on bringing a multifaceted mode of democratic pluralism into close alignment with active egalitarianism. By "multifaceted," I mean a world in which, first, a large variety of identities, faiths, and interests engage one another in the public square; second, periodic injections of new drives to the pluralization of faiths and rights rattle some of the old balances; and third, a positive ethos of engagement finds ample expression across these differences through the interinvolvements between public philosophy, policy priorities, and affective connections.

I also support drives to the radical reform of capitalism without having a clean recipe in hand to replace capitalism as such. I am not certain that anybody else has such a recipe either, during an era when the previous concentration of the working class in large factories and mines has been broken down into more dispersed, variegated, and less organized constituencies. The task is to stretch and strain capitalism toward a political culture that is more pluralistic, democratic, and egalitarian. Could capitalism then morph into something else that draws democracy, plurality, equality, and eco-practices yet closer together? I hope so, but my thinking on that question is still in movement.

These tensions are negotiated by pursuing an interim agenda that stretches the established terms of capitalism as it directs democracy in a more egalitarian direction. I then project plural socialism as something to pursue over the longer term. I also find myself concluding that a more widely distributed anger that must not be avowed about the unavoidable decline of America in the world plays an important role in the rather wide reach of the Trump phenomenon. That is one reason the undeliverable promise to return to a past that never was can carry power across classes. The intimately related reason is that the slogan promises a return to a less cluttered era of white triumphalism.

It is thus a dangerous time. My sense is that the best hope to make reasonable adjustments to American decline and the Anthropocene will emerge as pluralists come to terms more actively with the real grievances of the working and lower middle classes at the same time that we resist manifestations of racism and patriarchy emanating from sections of those classes. Is that more than a hope? I am unsure. Sometimes I think that the tensions and binds I encounter reflect unresolved knots in my thinking. At others I suspect they reflect binds in a world that does not necessarily escape tragic possibility. Because I also think that a demand for purity often backfires—the purities of morality, community, race, markets, individualism—I allow such indecisions and worries to find expression as the study proceeds.

This text was written before the events in Charlottesville, Virginia, on August 12, 2017. It goes into production a few days after that event. In Charlottesville, a pugnacious group of neo-Nazis, white supremacists, and Ku Klux Klan members demonstrated against the city's decision to take down the statue of Robert E. Lee, general of the Confederacy. Their message was racist and fascistic. They were looking for a fight. Many white triumphalists were armed, in a state that allows "open arms carry"; one drove his car into counterprotesters, killing one young woman and injuring numerous others. President Trump first condemned the violent racists along with "many others" who had demonstrated against them; later, he read in a passive voice a condemnation that focused on the neo-Nazis or "whatever you want to call them"; soon he took back the second statement to condemn all sides again, along with the "fake news media" who refused to pretend that the opponents of neo-Nazism are equivalent to its agents. As far as I know, none of the people who ended up in the hospital were members of the neo-Nazi contingent. Trump's message of moral equivalency encourages the kind of vigilante violence it purports to criticize. Clearly the most virulent section of his "base" who welcomed the last message saw it that way. They surely recall how their hero launched his political career by propagating the false narrative for six years that Barack Obama—the first African American president—was an illegitimate president because he was born in Kenya. They surely recall how he said he had agents in Hawaii who would prove this fact "very soon, believe me."

Donald Trump does teach us one thing: the beliefs you propagate have a lot to do with the quality of the dispositions you cultivate.

The event and his responses to it place us in a dangerous situation. It is heartwarming to see his popularity decline and to see more citizens become active against the viciousness of Trumpism. It is crucial, too, to recall how the resistance of the military and some corporations to Trumpist nativism is itself a product of pluralizing struggles over the past several decades that pressed those very institutions so hard to become more diverse. It is also true, however, that this impetuous, narcissistic leader remains in charge of a huge bureaucracy that now takes pernicious action on multiple fronts every day. He will be tempted to take yet more dangerous action to divert attention from how this one ripped off a tattered mask that had already slipped down. Aspirational fascists are destructive in their impulses and dangerous to the world in their acts.

Surely new events will unfold before this book sees the light of day. What is offered here, then, is incomplete, even from the perspective of a study with a genealogical ambition rather than one to historical completeness. Nonetheless, I hope that this report on engagements in one seminar with texts by Neumann, Arendt, Marcuse, Hitler, Adorno, Bataille, Freud, Timothy Mason, Norbert Elias, and Klaus Theweleit—a seminar also sprinkled here and there with clips from Hitler and Trump—does some work to help clarify the present.

Each session began with a student presentation comparing the text to be examined that week to themes and issues posed by earlier readings. We typically reserved the last half hour to talk about affinities and differences between the early stages of the Hitler movement and aspirational fascism today. I extend my respect and appreciation to Colin Eubank, Brian Caldwell, Tristan Klingelhoefer, Jacob Kripp, Michael McCreary, Ines Rerbal, Franziska Strack, and Yuanhai Zhu—all students in that seminar— for the thoughtful and exploratory character of their contributions. Franziska deserves double thanks for the superb role she played in preparing film clips and otherwise helping to move the seminar along.

I also thank Nidesh Lawtoo, Davide Panagia, Mort Schoolman, and Jane Bennett for the insightful comments each has made on key sections of this study.

The Rhetorical Strategies of Hitler and Trump

Genealogy and Fascism

My project is to contribute to a genealogy of fascism. Such a gene-alogy has at least three components. First, it strives to search the past in ways that might illuminate or crystallize specific tenden-cies and possibilities in the present. Second, it does that in part by showing how a series of practices often taken to be relatively con-stant or on a stable trajectory over time—say, sovereignty, the state, capitalism, morality, or democracy—is often enough composed of a series of heterogeneous elements with potentialities to shift in this way or that after a new shock or infusion. They have some-times become assembled together in more fragile ways than what appears at first glance. Here is one thing Nietzsche says about the evolution of a now rather stable assemblage, such as a religion, a state, a practice of punishment, a practice of sovereignty, a species, or a spe-cific constellation of climate and civilization, all the components of which are both interlinked and set on different time scales: "the cause of the origin of a thing and its eventual utility, its actual employment and place in a system of purposes, lie worlds apart; whatever exists, having somehow come into being, is again and again reinterpreted to new ends, taken over, transformed, and redirected by some power superior to it: all events in the organic world are a subduing, a becom-ing master, and all subduing and becoming master involves a fresh interpretation, an adaptation through which any previous 'meaning' and 'purpose' are necessarily obscured or even obliterated."[1]

1. Friedrich Nietzsche, *On the Genealogy of Morals,* trans. Walter Kaufmann (New York: Vintage Books, 1967), 77.

So several trajectories come replete with simmering potentialities that may break periodically in a variety of ways, even though the possibilities are constrained by the platform from which they proceed and specific situations encountered. Thus a fact is real, in that it exists in the world and makes a difference to other facts. You don't allow either fascists or wild-eyed constructivists—if any constructivists are indeed that wild—to say that all facts are ghostly, subjective, or "fake," depending on which ones pass the register of political acceptability. So, someone might insist either that the sun rotates around the earth or that the classical Newtonian theory fits the way of the way of the world itself. But in the first case, a Newtonian theory well grounded in evidence of multiple sorts can be invoked to correct that insistence. In the second, tests involving electrons forming wave patterns in a two-slit experiment and evidence of instant entanglement between particles now separated by millions of miles can be invoked to correct it. To be objective in these two cases means to conform to the most refined theory available in relation to tests with the most sophisticated instruments. This means, however, that something in the objective grasp of things may later shift, through a paradigm shift in theory, new powers of perception (say, Buddhist contemplation), and/or new tests with more refined instruments. But such a possibility, as already noted, does not reduce fact to subjective opinion. It is an objective fact that the earth revolves around the sun, as Spinoza knew when he invoked it to correct the common sense of his day founded on regular perception that the sun rotates around the earth.

But Nietzsche and Alfred North Whitehead also claimed that a fact is often more than itself; it both exists and may harbor incipiencies that could form new conjunctions with other forces on the way. A genetic mutation may simmer with diverse possibilities; some rather than others may surface when it encounters the specificity of an unfolding embryo. A student may be open to several theoretical perspectives; one may become consolidated out of that simmering facticity in ways that push others into obscurity. Conversion experiences help to show us how complex shifts in facticity are possible, with Paul, Augustine, Galileo, Nietzsche, and Whitehead providing excellent examples. Nietzsche was the devout son of a Lutheran minister who was expected to become a minister himself. His father died when he was young, and a series of other jolts opened up new possibilities of being. Whitehead was an obdurate supporter of Newtonian mechanics until the shock of quantum theory eventually pressed him to construct process philosophy.

Nietzsche's genealogy was thus designed to disjoin experimentally complex assemblages that others had tended to treat as universals that form a solid block of practices, or the unquestionable starting point of inquiry, or the implicit end point toward which things point. He loosened up our awareness of this or that assemblage so that we could sense how it might become reorganized through a combination of shocks from the outside and internal adjustments. If we extrapolate just a bit from the way he intended his notion of "will to power" to apply to both human and nonhuman force fields, we can say that his genealogies support a rather rhizomatic philosophy of time as a series of bumpy and intersecting becomings between diverse trajectories moving at different speeds and degrees of complexity. It is not a wild extrapolation to include such diverse trajectories as climate change, species evolution, glacier flows, Christian civilization, Buddhism, Kantianism, imperial expansions, and European democracy on the list of diverse trajectories. Any trajectory could begin to move more rapidly than heretofore or, through heterogeneous injections from elsewhere, become other to its previous self. Nietzsche thus resisted the theme of a linear trajectory of time—which he held to be a faulty, subjective opinion of his day. That is why, to him, Christianity, logical empiricism, Kantian morality, hermeneutics, and stringent forms of rationalism are all insufficient to themselves. Foucault, agreeing with this much in Nietzsche, constructed genealogies of madness, social discipline, sexuality, hermeneutics, normality, medical practice, and neoliberalism, while drawing sustenance from these forays to revise the direction and onto-sources of the ethic he pursued.

Well, the third dimension of genealogy is a quest for sources, norms, strategies, and dispositions worthy of embrace in the current setting. For instance, you may study past formations to promote intelligent modes of resistance to a repressive condition or to revise a series of regulative ideals from the past that continue to compete with each other in the present, doing the latter because you now discern a few complementarities between those contenders when you had seen only divergences before or, similarly, if you now think a new conjuncture requires reorganization of smooth ideals inherited from the past that now slide closer to specters.

A genealogy can thus encourage you to look again at contending ideals, such as neoliberalism, individualism, liberalism, and communism, doing so to highlight possible complementarities between some of them that had been obscure before. You don't necessarily reject everything in each. You may, rather, selectively disaggregate elements in it in the interests of reaggregating them in a new way. If those terms of art sound too mechanistic, you can say that new elements are injected into old swarms or assemblages in the hope that the latter will morph in this way or that. For to genealogists of the sort pursued here, both mechanistic models of explanation and organic models of interpretation—having competed with each other unevenly for hegemony in Euro-American thought for many centuries—are inadequate to a world composed of multiple, intersecting trajectories that may move slowly for a while and then accelerate.

Well, the ambition of this study is merely to instigate a genealogy of aspirational fascism in present-day America, doing so to think more reflectively about the distinctive conjuncture of diverse grievances, institutions, events, energies, and drives today, where, to take the key instance, a specific assemblage has formed between a rich, corrupt president, a large segment of the corporate and financial estate, many Republican Party leaders who had previously espoused a neoliberal ideology of autonomous market processes joined to a supportive state, an evangelical movement, and a distinctive segment of the white working and middle classes

who plug into the older assemblage with ambitions t
parties involved, to varying degrees, carry ugly pla
grants, Muslims, working women, urban areas, clima
tion, African Americans, Hispanics, urban life, and se
outside the United States.

One more thing about genealogy as I grapple with it: it is insufficient to sink into the discourses, representations, and ideologies
of the day, though each of these is relevant. You join those engagements to explorations of subliminal, affective modes of cultural
communication that stretch below the linguistic register as they
inject energies into it, and you focus on characteristic bodily disciplines and selective modes of attunement active within different
segments of the populace. These modes can be organized and expressed through aggressive styles of walking; violent street talk;
sharp rhythms of address; techniques of manipulation; instruments of control applied to others, such as those in prisons; barbed
wire or street surveillance cameras; tough bodyguards; rallies of
vilification; martial music; heroic cinematic scenes; standing at
attention; repeated *Heils* to an authoritarian leader; impersonal
architectural design; specific eating habits; and modes of vigilante
violence. The latter violences, for instance, intimidate or outrage
target constituencies, and they also harden the visceral register of
cultural life among vigilantes and ardent sympathizers.

A genealogy of fascism thus addresses multiple resonances between words, techniques, bodily demeanor, facial expressions,
fears, images, music, modes of empathy, bodily filters against sympathy, violence, and vilification, as it also seeks to open alternative
modes of creative receptivity and positive attraction.

According to a genealogical perspective with democratic aspirations, you don't fend off destructive affective dispositions merely by rising above them to a higher sphere of private and public
reflection. That helps for sure. But you also do so by encouraging
thought-imbued tendencies of presumptive responsiveness to become infused into the less refined registers of private and public
life. That is why genealogy is irreducible to merely representative

nking and textual analysis, even though they are involved. That is why the genealogists noted earlier thought about their own styles of speaking and writing as well as the formal modes of argumentation they practice. Hitler did too, in a different key.

Rhetorical Strategies

I will focus more closely on these latter issues in the next chapter. My agenda now is to drill down into how the Trumpian politics of persuasion is joined to shock politics: first, to think about the rhetorical power of the Trump phenomenon, second, to introduce counterrhetorical skills that may be needed today, and, third, to ask, in a preliminary way to be taken up later, how to fold a larger section of the white working class into active pluralizing movements that have recently and largely forsaken them. Radicals, liberals, and democrats have recently ceded large sections of the white working class to Trump and to the evangelical/capitalist resonance machine that preceded him. I treat it as axiomatic and essential that countermovements of today must oppose exploitative race and class hierarchies with demands for sharp reductions in inequality, must counter the aggressive white territorial nationalism of Trump with a politics of pluralism and pluralization, and must counter the aggressive leadership principle pursued (in different ways) by Trump, Putin, Le Pen, Hitler, and Lenin with multitiered horizontal communications, charismatic democratic leadership, care for the earth, and concerted efforts to address class, race, and gender hierarchies.

But in pursuing these strategies, it is important not to downplay the ubiquitous role of affective contagion in cultural life or even to reduce affective contagion to a force that only unruly masses succumb to through mediation of an authoritarian leader. The first response misses the phenomenon. The second may fear it so much that it pretends that affective contagion can be eliminated from public life in a democratic society. But the latter agenda is impossible because affective communication is, in some mode or other, a ubiquitous part of cultural life.

This is both a slippery and an essential topic. Those who pursue it run several risks; yet those who fail to engage it run even more. What is meant by "affective communication" will emerge gradually as we walk through Trump's tactics and, later, address the grievances and bodily practices that attune a constituency to specific modes of contagion while arming them to ward off others.

Perhaps we can gain preliminary bearings by listening to things Hitler said about the potent mixture of leadership, propaganda, and violence he commended and pursued in *Mein Kampf,* a two-part book published in 1926 and 1927, when the Nazi movement was consolidating itself in Germany. When I have mentioned this text to others, it has become clear that it is one of the widely unread texts of our time, both in Germany and the United States. New to me, too. I consult it now not because Trump is on a course that must end in death camps, or because the scapegoats he attacks are the same as those marked by Hitler, or because the institutional restraints against Trumpism are as weak as those earlier in place against Hitlerism, or because Hitler launched a world war and Donald Trump will necessarily lead to nuclear winter. The latter is indeed possible. But real differences between the two leaders, the circumstances propelling them, and the drives inspiring their movements can be kept in mind as we also probe certain affinities of style, tactics, and organization between them.

Trump, I want to say, is not a Nazi. He is, rather, an aspirational fascist who pursues crowd adulation, hyperaggressive nationalism, white triumphalism, a law-and-order regime giving unaccountable power to the police, a militarist, and a practitioner of a rhetorical style that regularly creates fake news and smears opponents to mobilize support for the Big Lies he advances. His internal targets of vilification and intimidation include Muslims, Mexicans, the media, the judiciary, independent women, the professoriate, and (at least early on) the intelligence services. The affinities across real differences between Hitler and Trump allow us to explore patterns of insistence advanced by Hitler in the early days of his movement to help illuminate the Trump phenomenon today.

Franz Neumann, in his profound, early study of German Nazism, said that democracy is both a bulwark against fascism and a precondition of its emergence. For to strive to introduce authoritarianism into a regime that has already tasted democratic elections, progressive social movements, and a plurality of autonomous social forces means that you need to draw a large segment of the population actively into the aggressive movement itself.[2] Fascism twists and distorts democracy while retaining its imperative to seek a mass basis. It mobilizes and organizes the popular support it needs, and it seeks to render the lines between consent and imposition blurry. Fake news is its stock in trade, and corollary charges of fake news against evidence-based claims become its premium stock. It thus depends on mobilizing intensive mass energies to sustain itself as it weakens the media, controls intelligence, curtails the autonomy of plural associations, and either eliminates or constricts the integrity of electoral politics.

My sense is that some comparisons between Hitler and Trump may illuminate affinities in their rhetorical styles, incitements to violence, strategies of affective contagion, and mobilization of a mass base. The first came to power without a majority vote, and the second was the beneficiary of a quasi-legal coup involving a weak candidate from the Democratic Party, a well-timed FBI intervention by Director Comey against her candidacy, a massive Putin computer intervention in the election, and the probable collusion of the Trump campaign with that intervention. The most apt comparison, then, may be between Hitler's rhetorical and organizational style in the early stages of his movement and Trumpism as the latter campaigned during the 2016 election and seeks to consolidate the reins of official power during the early stages of his presidency. Another pertinent difference between Hitler and Trump is that the former wrote directly about how to move crowds, whereas the latter has not.

2. Franz Neumann, *Behemoth: The Structure and Practice of National Socialism, 1933–1944,* trans. Peter Hayes (New York: Ivan R. Dee, 2009).

Here, then, are a few things Hitler said several years before the Nazi movement attained power:

The function of propaganda is, for example, not to weigh and ponder the rights of different people, but exclusively to . . . serve our own right, always and unflinchingly.

But here too there must be no half measures; the gravest and most ruthless decisions will have to be made. It is a half-measure to let incurably sick people steadily contaminate the remaining healthy ones.

Not vanity about fine clothes which everyone cannot buy, but vanity about a beautiful, well-shaped body which everyone can help to build. . . . If physical beauty were not forced entirely into the background of our foppish fashions, the seduction of hundreds of thousands of girls by bow-legged, repulsive Jewish bastards would not be possible.

It belongs to the genius of a great leader to make even adversaries far removed from one another seem to belong to a single category, because in weak and uncertain characters the knowledge of having different enemies can only too readily lead to the beginning of doubt in their own right.

Only a Knowledge of the Jews provides the key with which to comprehend the inner and consequently real, aims of Social Democracy. . . . The erroneous conceptions of the aim and meaning of this party fall from our eyes like veils, once we come to know this people.

I gradually so transformed myself into a speaker for mass meetings, that I became practiced in the pathos and the gestures which a great hall with its thousands of people demands.

For the bourgeoisie and the intelligentsia protest against such a view [of propaganda] because they themselves lack the power and ability to influence the masses by the spoken word, since they have thrown themselves more and more into purely literary activity and renounced the agitational activity of the spoken word.

He will always let himself be borne by the great masses in such a way that instinctively the very words come to his lips that he needs to speak to the hearts and minds of his audience.

If he suspects that they do not seem convinced of the soundness of his argument, repeat it over and over with constantly new examples.

[When a mass rally succeeds,] he himself has succumbed to the magic influence of what we designate as "mass suggestion," The will, the longing, and also the power of thousands are accumulated in every individual.

[At a Marxist disruption of a Nazi meeting,] in a few seconds the whole hall was filled with a roaring, screaming crowd. The dance had not yet begun when my storm troopers—for so they were called from this day on—attacked. Like wolves they flung themselves in packs of eight or ten again and again on their enemies.

The committee sessions, of which minutes were kept and of which votes were taken, represented in reality a parliament on a small scale. When my appointment to the position as first chairman had given me the necessary authority, this nonsense immediately stopped.[3]

"Well-formed Aryan women," "always and unflinchingly," "the gravest and most ruthless decisions," "boundless wrath," "fanatical intolerance," Jews as a red thread "tying disparate enemies together," "pathos and gestures," "repeat it over and over," "the disconnection of university professors," "mass suggestion," "conquest of the streets," the "nonsense" of "parliamentarianism." The rhetorical and organizational affinities across significant differences in agenda, goals, scapegoats, and style between the two are multiple. Trump does not speak of Aryan women at his rallies; he parades them as unattainable objects of desire before his followers as he repeatedly castigates minorities and disabled people who do not meet the norms of beauty and normality he projects. That is why it fit the bill when Trump said about John McCain, the wounded Republican senator and prisoner during the Vietnam War, that he prefers his heroes to be uninjured and unwounded. He does not single out Jews as "the red thread" to tie disparate enemies together into one package, though some of his admirers do head in that direction. He treats Muslims as a thread tying to-

3. Adolf Hitler, *Mein Kampf,* trans. Ralph Manheim (New York: Houghton Mifflin, 1943), 182, 255, 412, 118, 51, 454, 468, 469, 469, 470, 471, 477, 479, 505, 543, 588.

gether wrath against several constituencies who resist the intense nationalism and white triumphalism he trumpets under the heading of "Make America Great Again," with the "Again" referring to a fictive picture of the 1950s before pluralizing movements in the United States became so active. McCarthyism, in fact, was a powerful movement in the 1950s that attacked the film industry, the State Department, labor, and the professoriate as hotbeds of communism. Trump incites fanatical intolerance against his own constituencies of choice: Muslims, Mexicans, the news media, feminists, African Americans, ecologists, the film industry, and the professoriate. Another affinity between Trump and Hitler deserves note. Trump has already become famous for his impetuousness, his narcissism, his instability, and his inability to pay attention at briefing sessions. And, as biographers of Hitler know, Hitler also was impetuous, impatient with briefings, and erratic in behavior.[4] Perhaps a larger study of how ruthlessness, narcissism, the demand for one-way loyalty, and grandiose projects can sometimes hang together in the same personality is needed today. One study we consult in chapter 2 starts down that path in its examination of "The Manipulative Personality."

Trump's speeches, replete with eerie echoes to those of Hitler, are delivered with grandiose bodily gestures, grimaces, Big Lies, hysterical charges, dramatic repetitions, and totalistic assertions that only he can clean up the "mess." The repetitions, supported almost every day by tweets, function as signals that allow his fans to hear a cluster of claims each time any one signal is repeated.

He often confides to supporters at rallies that he would like to beat up protesters, and during his 2016 campaign (which is now becoming interminable), he repeatedly urged the crowd to turn and scream at the media "scavengers" and "scum" assembled be-

---

4. One study that pursues that issue with respect to Hitler is Volker Ullrich, *Hitler's Ascent, 1889–1939* (New York: Alfred Knopf, 2016). I thank Mort Schoolman for recently calling it to my attention. This book is full of riches relevant to our topic.

hind them. If a constituency is "scum," there are no limits to what can be done to them at night when no one is watching. His personal guards tolerate no protest and are rough on peaceful protesters, often inciting people in the crowd to take violent action of their own. And, at least in aspiration, he joins aggressive speeches to a shock politics of rapid-fire executive orders to keep the world roiling.

In the early stages of his campaign, the media, pundits, and professoriate often underplayed the power of Trumpian rhetoric and shock tactics to incite its key target audience: an aggrieved white working and lower middle class that had too often been treated as huddled under a flyover zone by liberals and radicals in ways that elide the lived struggles they face and the compensatory attachments that tempt them. This latter constituency has been caught for several decades in a squeeze between neoliberal practices of escalating inequality and worker insecurity, on one side, and noble pluralizing drives, on the other side, that fail to identify the white working class—many residing in deindustrialized Rust Belt states—to be one of the struggling minorities in need of support. The distinctive bind into which this constituency is caught primes many in it to open valves of responsiveness to Trump as he intensifies and channels their anger along specific canals.

Some pundits, especially early in the Republican primaries, made fun of Trump's speaking style. I hesitate to do so, at least in a dismissive way. His style is not designed first and foremost to articulate a policy agenda. It draws energy from the anger of its audience as it channels it. It draws into a collage dispersed anxieties and resentments about deindustrialization, race, border issues, immigration, working-class insecurities, trade policies, pluralizing drives, the new place of the United States in the global economy, and tacit uncertainty about the shaky place of a neoliberal culture on this planet. The speech montages then transfigure these anxieties into anger as they identify convenient targets of outlet for that anger. Trump's animated gestures, facial expressions, finger pointing, strutting, signature phrase clusters, and recurrent twirls around the stage to call out the roaring acclaim of the audience amplify the words he recites. They incite and direct anxiety into anger as they recall a time in America in which white triumphalism felt secure. Each element in a Trump performance flows and folds into the others until an aggressive resonance machine is formed that is more intense than its parts.

The montage deepens anger and focuses positive identification upon an authoritarian, narcissistic figure who aspires to squash critics and solicit unquestioned acclaim from subordinates and followers. That is why "loyalty" is always a one-way street for Trump. In these speeches, you can hear strains of a cultural melancholy that must not be openly articulated: "Make America Great, Again." Hitler responded to a world in which Germany had been defeated, was blocked in its imperial drives, had passed through a horrendous inflationary spiral, and soon confronted the ravages of the Great Depression. Trump responds to one in which old imperial and racist practices soaked in deniability have encountered deindustrialization and new troubles for recently entitled white working and middle classes. The differences between the two regimes and times are very large, to be sure, but strange echoes are discernible enough to render it feasible to explore how the campaigns of the latter express affinities to the rhetorical strategies of the former.

One reason that the most ardent Trump supporters so far demand so little from him with respect to values they themselves often propagate about marital life, church attendance, clean speech, and respect for the disabled is because they are tempted to concur with his demand that the Leader be exempt from limits ordinary people are called upon to acknowledge. Another is how the Lies he tells provide them, too, with hooks upon which to hang several grievances. Another yet is how those standards are often projected upon women rather than men. Such a combination may help to explain the surprise journalists often report when they confront supporters about their tolerance of Trump behavior that they would often not accept in other public figures.[5] Beyond that, a highly dangerous minority, mobilized into dark vigilante and trolling clusters, loves Trump's behavior and seeks to exacerbate it.

One cluster of demeaning associations in a Trump speech draws together the dangers of assertive femininity, minority standing, non-Christian religions, disability, foreignness, weakness, vulnerability, and dissolution so that each item on that line vibrates with perceived threats posed by the others: now the whole line resonates together. Thus Trump's apparent lapses in sharpness of argument or linear flow are in fact crucial to the rhetorical style he forges. Later, when followers hear any of the items to oppose recited by a Trump critic, they can associate its bearer with every sin on the list. Critics spouting objections to a particular item can now be lumped together under the rubric of "political correctness," a stopgap phrase designed to halt receptive communication with suspects outside the core movement. Of course, it helps Trump if some advocates of identity politics press a large litany of accusations against the working class without also paying attention to the grievances that help to render them susceptible to Trump.

The line of negative associations repeatedly tied together by Trump is then treated as if it can only be overcome by a positive line between alpha masculinity, ultra-self-assertion, compliant women, violent gestures, impermeable territorial walls, an aggressive unitary nation, and police and military ruthlessness against losers. That is one reason Trump keeps referring to such alpha-male symbols as Putin, tough-talking miners, veterans, generals, and the police. These formulations are punctuated by recurrent use of vague, positive terms that purport to describe but actually obfuscate or project: "it will be beautiful," "people say," "someone

5. For one gripping account of how and why the leader is exempt from the standards enforced upon the followers in such a movement, see Sigmund Freud, *Group Psychology and the Analysis of the Ego,* trans. James Strachey (New York: W. W. Norton, 1959). We engage his theory of crowd behavior in the next chapter.

said," "a loyal American," "believe me," and "nobody knew" are favorite tics. "Believe me" is often invoked when he is lying and invoking authority over his followers. "Nobody knew" is a Trump projection with thin cover, saying that nobody knew health care was complex or that France was the first ally of the United States when in fact he did not know until recently.

The hyperaggressive self and the triumphant nation are now called upon to erect the same sharp boundaries, replete with powerful filters against receptive attention to other perspectives or places. That is how Trump's image of the aggressive individual and the triumphant, walled nation fit together. The filters, in turn, are to be lowered only to receive new infusions from the leader. Luckily, this latter of Trump's aspirations is still not fulfilled by most citizens.

Trump has thus become a relatively skilled rhetorician of a new aspirational fascism, not a failed teacher or public speaker. Father Coughlin (with a radio audience of 30 million), Joseph McCarthy, George Wallace, Pat Buchanan, Ann Coulter, Sean Hannity, and Sarah Palin, true enough, preceded him, and indeed helped to pave the way for him. But none of them captured the reins of the state, with its extensive war-making power, court appointments, Bully Pulpit, executive orders, and surveillance apparatus under their official control. Given the propitious circumstances for the movement Trump foments, we are perhaps lucky he is not more skilled. And that so far, a variety of institutions and protesting movements have risen to combat the threat he poses.

Affective Contagion

It is pertinent to highlight how the affective contagion Trump propagates infuses the visceral register of cultural life among target constituencies. That register is itself often marked by conceptual cloudiness and affective intensities on the move that can be selectively open to coding as they enter into spiral communications with more refined registers of reflection and communication.[6] The aggressive gestures, simplifications, Lies, shouts, repetitions, grimaces, triumphant circling to register acclaim, and thinly veiled threats emanating from Trump help to code the visceral register in ways that do not work as effectively outside a crowd setting or mass TV audience. Late-night tweets, extreme executive orders, warnings against those who resist, and aggressive Hannity interviews are then deployed to keep the momentum alive. The tweets continue to stoke anxiety, transfiguring it into anger against convenient figures and constituencies. The chosen targets serve as pegs because attacks on them do not demand serious changes in the interlocking orders of democracy and capitalism in ways that would actually speak to defining problems of the day. The targets appear vulnerable, the answers easy, if a strong leader assumes power.

Followers now become inflamed when they hear counterarguments against Trump offered by reporters, comedians, pundits, liberals, and professors. Put one way, Trumpian rhetoric, crowd organization, and shock tactics help to consolidate specific thought-imbued memes into the habitus of followers as they simultaneously create blocks against attending to discordant facts and perspectives. The blockages are as important as the inflammations.

6. So it is wise to bypass those who say that "affect theory" defines affect to be thought free, is grounded in simple determinism, denies intentionality or agency, ignores the intersubjective dimension of cultural life, or treats the brain like a layered cake. (The layered cakes I have eaten don't foster spiral communications between diverse body–brain registers operating at different speeds and degrees of thought-imbued, affective intensity as they receive and synthesize multimodal messages from the world.) Because many theorists of affective contagion support "panexperientialism," in which many beings outside humanity are said to be equipped with variable degrees of feeling, agency, and creativity, the misrepresentations in such portrayals can be breathtaking. Jane Bennett explores the quiet power of sympathetic, horizontal, affective communications in a book now in preparation.

The crowds who love Trump also rebel against the apparent hegemony established elites give to the written over the oral, the refined over the vernacular, the representational over the performative, and the calm over the agitational. The first item in each pair becomes identified with "the establishment" or "liberals on the two coasts."

Because there is never in actuality a vacuum on the visceral register of cultural life, the difficult task now becomes how to respond to Trumpism on all of the visceral and refined registers of cultural communication, perception, and action-oriented judgment. That is why I do not only laugh at the Trump rhetorical style but also seek to study it so as to devise multiform strategies to counter it. He stumbles often, but he is not reducible to the stumbling, bumbling character some, at least early on, made him out to be. In fact, to call him that is to enrage key male constituents who often identify with the style, tone, and demeanor he displays. His own thinly veiled vulnerabilities form part of that power, as we shall see more closely in the next chapter.

At the right moments, however, laughter and satire in tandem with effective exposés can do noble work, as Steve Colbert, *Saturday Night Live,* Sarah Silverman, Jimmy Kimmel, and, earlier, Jon Stewart have taught us. These exaggerations, freeze-framings, and satirical repetitions bring out both how Trump works his crude magic on the visceral register of chosen constituents and how his clownish character could eventually become something to resist. Some satires may be anchored in the assumption that affective communication must always be transcended, while others grasp how it must be reformed as well as transcended. The latter are profound, as they show how there is never a vacuum on the visceral register of affective communication. We are also lucky that innumerable citizens today teach each other how the Trump strategy is designed, thereby enabling us to counter it more effectively. We must, for instance, forewarn each other how future Trump stumbles are apt to be followed by the creation or use of shocking events to intimidate critics and spur his base. You can

call this the Reichstag temptation, one that tempts Trump each
and every time a stumble is made.

One agenda for the future is to study further how the rhetorical styles of Hitler, Trump, Putin, Le Pen, and other narcissistic
leaders work in relation to the shock tactics they favor (and practice when they can). As we do so, we will also need to heed the
rhetorical counterpowers of talented democratic speakers like, in
the United States at least, Cornel West, Bernie Sanders, William
Barber, Elizabeth Warren, and (sometimes) Barack Obama. The
latter figure campaigned with democratic eloquence but governed with bookish reticence—in the face of an extremely hostile
Republican Congress, U.S. Supreme Court, and many state govern-
ments. Trump, we can be confident, will be a perpetual campaign-
er as long as he remains in office, enacting those aggressive skills
as he seeks to pull the Court, the FBI, the CIA, local police forces,
Fox News, the neoliberal elite, and a mélange of vigilante groups
more securely into his orbit. He admires Putin so much, in part,
because the latter combines the politics of the Big Lie with the use
of *kompromat* and police violence to imprison, torture, or murder
those who challenge him. I leave open whether the FBI will be
able to maintain enough integrity to complete its investigation of
the highly probable collusion between the Trump campaign and
Putin.

The Big Lie Scenario

I do not see the current conjuncture as a revolutionary moment
for the democratic Left, even though the continuation of protests,
unruly town hall meetings, court challenges, blog posts, and public
satires form critical parts of the resistance. I do, indeed, fear that it
could become a revolutionary moment for a fascist Right, though
that is not inevitable. Putin, for instance, could derail Trump by
covertly releasing materials that show how compromised he is. Or
the FBI investigation could bear so much fruit that a Republican
Congress can no longer deflect it. Or Trump could collapse through

an inordinate mistake. It is, nonetheless, an extremely dangerous time. My comments, incomplete and preliminary, are couched within such a general understanding. These thoughts may sound irrelevant to those who continue to think that affective contagion is something only to overcome rather than also to counter on the visceral register of cultural life.

Trumpian persuasion draws significantly upon the repetition of Big Lies. A Big Lie, such as the birther charge against Obama, the first African American president; the assertion to have seen "thousands of Muslims" on TV celebrate 9/11 when there were no such celebrations; the campaign charge that the 2016 election was rigged; the false repetition that he won by a landslide; the constant refrain that the media always lies about him; the persistent denial or deflection of Putin election hacking; the promise that Mexico will pay for the Wall; the claim that climate change is a Chinese hoax; the eventual take back of the birther charge after several years of insistence matched by the assertion that the Hillary Clinton campaign had started it; the charge that Obama had wiretapped Trump Tower; the assertion that his first hundred days in office have been the most productive ever—are all designed to provide his aggrieved constituency with acceptable pegs upon which to hang the sources of their real grievances and resentments as they also deny the urgent need of America to adjust to its new position in the world and its vulnerable relation to a series of large planetary forces.[7] No Lie must speak to the need for structural shifts in the character of American capitalism, modes of

---

7. In a June 21, 2017, speech in Iowa, the *New York Times* reviewed twelve Trump falsehoods cheered wildly by the crowd. They included the claim that the United States is the highest taxed nation in the world (it is number 22 in corporate tax revenue and lower for general tax revenue as a percentage of gross domestic product), false claims about the Paris climate agreement, and a promise to bar immigrants from receiving welfare benefits for five years (that law was on the books before he took office). "An Adoring Crowd and a Dozen Things That Aren't True," *New York Times,* June 23, 2017, A20.

consumption and response to galloping climate change; each must concentrate the real grievances of the constituency upon vulnerable targets as they fuel the Great Denial flowing underneath them.

Each time a Big Lie is repeated, we must join factual corrections of it to a more general account of how the Big Lie Scenario works and what modes of deniability it seeks to protect.[8] Factual correction alone is not enough. You must show how repetition of the Scenario creates pegs, helps to code the visceral register of anger, and channels the resentments of aggrieved constituencies, even when many Trump supporters themselves doubt the Lie on the more refined registers of reflective belief. You must show how it aims to divert attention from other responses to real grievances. Often enough, a new Big Lie is introduced when new evidence about Trump's own participation in collusion or corruption is about to come forth, as when his charge that the election was being rigged was shouted out just before Rudi Giuliani intimated to Fox News that a new intervention in the election was about to arrive from the FBI. It did arrive very soon from Director Comey. Or the charge that the media is "the enemy of the people" was touted just when new evidence about the Trump–Putin collusion was about to go public. Or the repeated charge that CNN reports "fake news," which started shortly after some blog sites Trump draws on had been shown to manufacture news claims out of nothing. The idea here is to cauterize public outrage by making it seem that "both sides" say the same thing about the other. A closely related strategy is to concentrate bombastically on the foolish claim that the Iran deal was a travesty to draw attention from the fact that he

8. For one earlier account of how the Big Lie works, see Connolly, "Donald Trump and the New Fascism," *The Contemporary Condition* (blog), August 14, 2016, http://contemporarycondition.blogspot.com/search/label /William%20E.%20Connolly. For a more extensive discussion of the role of satire in exposing and countering the work of these scenarios, see Nidesh Lawtoo and William E. Connolly, "Rhetoric, Fascism and the Planetary," *The Contemporary Condition* (blog), July 2017, http://contemporarycondition .blogspot.com/2017/07/rhetoric-fascism-and-planetary.html.

refuses to take action to avoid the repetition of Russian interventions in American elections. The Big Lie Scenario is a strategy to undermine evidence-based claims, create false equivalencies, sow confusion, divert attention, promote acceptance of authoritarian rule, and legitimize a shock wave politics of rapid shifts.

Another ruse is eventually to give up a Big Lie when it no longer works or is not needed, doing so by placing responsibility for its origin on an opponent—as Trump did on the day he took it back that Clinton had started the birther controversy. Hitler pursued similar tactics, particularly during the early days of his regime.

Again, soon enough, Trump is apt to support Lies by taking advantage of a shocking event, as Hitler did early on with the Reichstag fire, the burning down of the Weimar legislative building that provided him with a pretext to establish permanent martial law. To expose the Big Lie Scenario, you must recite repeatedly how it works on the visceral register of culture over time to undermine a democratic culture of informed accountability, how the endless repetition of such Lies is linked intrinsically to the Reichstag temptation, and how a political culture based upon the rapid circulation of rumors ungrounded in evidence diverts attention from key issues as it hands increasing degrees of power to those who run the rumor machine.

It may be possible over time to negate the Big Lie Scenario. Why and how? Well, one reason is that the kind of rhetoric Trump practices combines intense attraction to him from supporters with a residual sense of repulsion against the terms of that identification. Part of the reason for this is the internal conflict in play between the dominant desire of an aggrieved constituency to give itself to the Trumpian crowd through identification with the leader and a residual desire to maintain a degree of self-autonomy joined to evidence-based claims.[9]

9. I note here a superb essay by Nidesh Lawtoo on the ambiguity of affective contagion, in which attraction and a residue of repulsion tend to come into play together. See Lawtoo, "The Mimetic Community: Revolting against (New) Fascism" (unpublished manuscript, 2017).

So counterrepetitions of just how the Big Lie Scenario works may help to prepare people for the day when that residual repulsion against authoritarianism surfaces. Another related reason is that many who voted for Trump were shaky in doing so. They were not that happy with either candidate. So they took a leap in the dark for the one they did not know rather than falling again for a safer, neoliberal democrat whose propensities to ignore them they knew all too well.

These considerations provide some reason to hope that while Trump supporters may resist exposés and countertactics in the early going, new events and future failures could encourage a larger segment of this constituency to allow previously suppressed doubts to crystallize. Such a delayed response, for instance, did occur during the Nixon years with respect to Watergate. Few had been willing to listen to the abundant evidence about Watergate until well after the Nixon–McGovern election. Later, polls reported that a large majority said they had voted for the Democrat—who had in fact lost by a historic margin. A similar combination occurred during the tenure of George W. Bush with respect to Iraq. As a critic of the Iraq War before it started, I participated in several large demonstrations, small vigils, and public postings shunned by most citizens at the time. There is reason to believe, however, that the shadowy doubts opened by the repetition of such actions by activists at multiple sites helped to sharpen the public rebuke against Bush and the war once it finally began to gather steam. It definitely helped to stiffen the backs of military dissidents and reporters who insisted upon reporting some of the horrific events during that war that the Bush administration tried so hard to cover up—a rapid crystallization of previously suppressed doubts.

Class and Charisma

It is pertinent to see how the white working and lower middle classes now sit on the razor's edge of time as they cope with the devastating effects of deindustrialization and the relative dearth of vibrant voices on the democratic Left who have spoken intensely to their grievances. My working-class sister—to cite one revealing instance—tried in November 2016 to organize an election night party among Democratic voters in the Flint, Michigan, area, only to find that most of her erstwhile Democratic friends had "sold out" to Trump. Her retired husband had a few years earlier been included with thousands of other GM retirees in forfeiting 40 percent of his monthly retirement income as part of a bankruptcy program to save General Motors. Innumerable other retired workers in several manufacturing corporations have faced similar, almost silent fates. There was way too little clamor about that devastating event, and others like it, from the democratic Left. I understand how ugly activities emanating from portions of this class can discourage attempts to appreciate its real grievances, as many of its members find themselves and their children moving from a relatively recent period of entitlement to one of greater insecurity and loss of confidence in a future that can speak to them. "Make America Great, Again" speaks viscerally to them. It is, to me, almost miraculous that my Flint-area relatives held out against the Trump machine after receiving little public support in opposing the silent injustices they and so many in their general situation have faced.

A huge cadre of the white working class supported Trump in the 2016 election. So did 82 percent of white evangelicals, a large portion of whom are located in the working and lower middle classes. But that crowd also contains a reserve of citizens who could turn against him if and when they see how he has conned them. This will be so, however, only if more critical voices outside the working class speak forcefully to its real grievances and suffering while simultaneously supporting other minorities in even more precarious and vulnerable positions.

We will explore more closely in chapter 3 how strategies to fold vibrant drives to egalitarianism into democratic pluralism could work to draw large sections of the white working and lower middle classes back into a pluralizing culture.

Such changes are valuable in themselves. They also promote intraclass connections across multiple minorities who would all benefit from them. Single mothers, working-class African Americans, same-sex couples in the working class, and lower-income minorities of all sorts who hold underwater mortgages and face retirement squeezes would benefit together from such general policies, setting the stage for formation of more positive connections. When pluralism is joined much more obdurately to class egalitarianism, it becomes both more noble and more resilient—particularly when a large corps of pluralist leaders in different positions develop and enact rhetorical skills bolstering the horizontal pulls of democratic life.

Would such changes ease the way for more working-class whites to accept the new position of America in the world, as they also overcome evasions of institutional racism and the galloping pressures of climate change? I do not know. I do know that many in these situations already resist such temptations, and I suspect that these new initiatives could increase the odds that such messages would be absorbed by a larger portion. It can also be hoped that more of those outside this class who are repelled by the strains of ugliness within this constituency will come to discern more closely the grievances that foster temptations to that ugliness. It is a shaky time.[10]

The ugliness finding ample expression today in sections of the white working class must no longer be deployed as a reason to ig-

10. One post by me in 2011 in the Contemporary Condition was called "Aspirational Fascism." It is now reprinted in *Common Dreams,* October 4, 2011, http://www.commondreams.org/views/2011/10/04 /aspirational-fascism. Some critics of my ideal of pluralism may have thought that it underplays the dangers of our time and makes pluralism sound too easy. I suggest that they consult chapter 3, "Fundamentalism in America," in my *An Ethos of Pluralization* (Minneapolis: University of Minnesota Press, 1995). The text also explores the need to bring pluralism and egalitarianism much closer together. Chapters 4 and 6 explore why drives to pluralization are so hard to promote with respect to African Americans and Amerindians in this society.

nore its actual grievances. The idea is to call out expressions of racism, militarism, climate denialism, and misogyny when you encounter them as you simultaneously demand positive responses to legitimate working-class grievances. Show how reasonable solutions to them are compatible with a pluralizing, egalitarian culture. The task is to define the pluralizing Left anew as an ally of the white working and lower middle classes as it simultaneously retains strong support for the rights and needs of other constituencies who are often suffering even more. The pluralizing Left, indeed, simmers with such potentiality.

Hopefully, it has become clear to more on the democratic Left how necessary it is to move a variety of pluralizing minorities closer to a larger segment of the working class. For the latter class, once you take into account relative income level, education level, type of work, degree of job security, relative income increases over a career, and declining retirement prospects, has itself become a minority. This becomes even more obvious when you discern how what was once a decent wage in the United States has now become less so as the infrastructure of consumption has evolved to make it more expensive to make ends meet than heretofore.[11] This is an aggrieved minority, too.

Hopefully, too, that clarity has not arrived too late to counter the hold Trump has gained over a large swath of this class, led by those on its evangelical, military, veteran, rural, and police edges. The Hillary Clinton campaign, again, missed the boat in this respect, even if the Democratic platform she was pressed to enact

11. I explore how an evolving infrastructure of consumption places pressures on the working and middle classes in Connolly, *Capitalism and Christianity, American Style* (Durham, N.C.: Duke University Press, 2008), chapter 4. So income figures, taken alone, are misleading; they become more so when you take into account relative job security, authoritarian bosses, educational opportunities, retirement options, mortgages pulled underwater by bad state policies, and health insurance costs. A classic text that captures this phenomenon in a complementary way is Fred Hirsch, *The Social Limits to Growth* (London: Blackwell, 1977).

by Bernie supporters—and supposed to represent in the election—made modest gestures in this direction.

If a dissident movement is to acquire momentum, the democratic Left must also identify more young leaders in multiple settings who are charismatic in democratic ways and who can inspire large constituencies as they counter the appeal of Trumpian authoritarian charisma. For Trump is a charismatic adversary whose rhetorical effectiveness has not yet been measured adequately by enough of his critics. He and Hitler are both right about one thing: there is a tendency in the professoriate to downplay the role of rhetoric in politics and the ubiquitous importance of the visceral register of culture to public life. We often love writing more than speech. There is thus a corollary reticence to working hard enough to counter a rhetoric organized around authoritarian leadership, militarism, whiteness, and aggressive national assertion with another mode that draws on our higher angels to encourage horizontal modes of organization and an ethos of presumptive generosity as it articulates the differential class, regional, and urban dangers of rapid climate change.

We both need to learn more about Trump and to rebut his rhetorical style with positive styles of engagement. Bernie Sanders shined a bright light here, too. For visceral group identifications do not always and only pass through the filter of a narcissistic leader, as a few steeped in Freudianism may think. They can also be mediated by horizontal connections on both the visceral and refined registers of cultural life—connections forged across a variety of associational meetings, church assemblies, blogs, family gatherings, classrooms, neighborhood groups, school boards, tavern conversations, unions, and so on—as we forge reciprocal ties of presumptive generosity and care.[12] Charismatic, pluralizing, egalitarian leaders support such horizontal connections and

12. If the visceral register of cultural life is ineliminable, and if pluralists must find ways to infuse it with presumptive generosity as it simultaneously works on the more refined registers of cultural life, the question of manipulation immediately rears its head. Here is one thing I said about

infusions in the ways they provide Democratic leadership.[13] It is possible to improve the internal ethos of the United States while coming to terms more nobly with its new condition in the world, even if the probabilities may point in another direction. Indeed, it is imperative to try to accomplish both together, because failure to do so risks unleashing the vast military power of the country in a series of destructive wars that could be calamitous for the world. Think merely of how climate change—a gathering planetary force massive in destructive power—is subject to denial in part because those who seek to return to an old "greatness" are told that such a return requires the modes of industry, mining, imperial power, triumphalism, and fossil fuel energy that powered growth the last time around.

Trump's attack upon the media and the professoriate is strategically chosen in this respect. His tweets calling the media "the enemy of the people" and carriers of "fake news" must never be treated lightly. Above all, this is not a site, if there is any site, at which the Left should seek to "accelerate the contradictions" of the order to speed up its collapse.[14] The latter route, however unintentionally, is a route to fascism.

---

this near-dilemma in an earlier essay: "How can one participate in such strategies without becoming an envoy of cultural manipulation? I support a three tiered strategy: You expose the tactics of those who don't themselves call attention to them; you introduce counter-strategies of cultural-corporeal infusion attached to a more generous vision of public life; and you publicize as you proceed how these counterstrategies themselves impinge upon the affectively rich, nonconscious layers of life." William E. Connolly, "Experience and Experiment," *Daedalus,* Summer 2006, 74.

13. Romand Coles, in *Visionary Pragmatism: Radical and Ecological Democracy in Neoliberal Times* (Durham, N.C.: Duke University Press, 2016), effectively charts strategies to generate a new counterresonance machine, one that works simultaneously on the visceral and refined registers of cultural life.

14. I concur with the critique of "accelerationism" advanced by Deborah Danowski and Eduardo Viveiros de Castro in *The Ends of the World* (Cambridge: Polity Press, 2017), 50–57. They say, "The accelerationalists basic intuition is that a certain world, which has already ended, must

Trump's goal is to trap the media in a bind: he hopes he can win if the media evades the charges he makes; he hopes he can win if they reply simply by correcting the evidence when he endlessly accuses them of fake news. The best strategy, perhaps, is to keep exposing how the Big Lie works, to respond with evidence-based claims to each Lie as you also explain why he pursues it, to play up dramatically how critical a press free from state control or intimidation is to a democratic society, and to explore the real and neglected grievances of those constituencies most tempted to embrace Trump tweets. Yes, the media often deserves intense criticism from the democratic Left for its softness on a neoliberal corporate culture, but the Left must also expose and attack Trumpian intimidation of it. It recently seemed unwise to me, for instance, when a few on the Left reenforced Trump and Putin denials of the Putin intervention in the election with statements that came close to describing this as fake news. The media and professoriate will both be vicious targets of Trump attacks for the next four years (at least), as he deflects attention from his probable collusion with Putin and the failure of his policies to uplift the working class. It is possible for critics on the Left to chew gum and walk at the same time, in this case, to hold the media accountable as you also defend it against vicious Trumpian assaults that could get worse as his false promises continue to encounter harsh realities.

I have doted a bit on the working class not because it could today become the center of a new movement toward egalitarian democracy oriented to both pluralism and the new planetary condition. We do not inhabit a Fordist era in which much of the working class is centered in large factories. That class is now even more dispersed geographically and underorganized into unions. It is often distributed in small clusters in fast-food

---

finish ending, that is, fully actualize its inexistence. . . . After the apocalypse, the Kingdom" (51).

restaurants, shopping mall stores, janitorial duties, farm work, small factories, prison work, security assignments, subordinate administrative duties, hospital services, and so on. Moreover, its dispersed distribution makes it easier for those outside those circumstances to ignore or deny its grievances, as they look merely at yearly income statistics and fail to register how differences in lifetime income and an evolving infrastructure of consumption make it harder for many with apparently decent incomes to make ends meet. Its very dispersion, disorganization, and uneven geo-distribution, however, mean that, intelligently engaged, it could also forge indispensable elements in a vibrant pluralism that has been on the move for a while without its active involvement, a pluralism that can also constitute a key bulwark against aspirational fascism. That is why it is wise to appreciate the working class today as one dispersed minority among others.

If and when we speak to the higher angels of the working class, we might help to consolidate a vibrant pluralist assemblage already in motion organized around several sexualities, diverse religious creeds, a few class positions, ethnicities, urban and rural locations, and "races"—all assembled in part to realize a better society and in part to defeat aspirational fascism.

There is little doubt that such an agenda faces deep difficulties of achievement in the United States, especially with respect to speaking to the grievances of African Americans and Native Americans. But that does not mean that the difficult drive to a more egalitarian pluralism should be scrapped in favor of a drive to a more centered nation. The latter agenda, as fascist perversions of it show, is both more dangerous and filled with its own exclusionary drives. It means, rather, that the struggle must both be intensified and rendered more creative. It is important to recall again that one hallmark of the early drives to fascism in Europe was the replacement of real diversity with a fraudulent plurality organized from the top down. Another was the tendency of private finance, large corporations, and market ideologues to endorse a fascist movement once it became powerful.[15] To them, the prospective alternatives were worse.

If and as an egalitarian pluralist assemblage becomes mobilized sufficiently to make impressive advances, it might then strive to transfigure the existing order into a distinctive kind of democratic socialism, one that places ecology, egalitarianism, plurality, and critical responsiveness to new constituencies high on the agenda.

I will focus on these issues in the last chapter, without claiming to give a definitive response to them. But before we get there, it is imperative to dig more deeply into how affective communication works and how specific regimes of relational bodily disciplines can open a constituency to some modes of rhetorical influence and insulate it against others. I do not claim we will grasp fully how the interplay between rhetoric and bodily discipline works. I do suggest that an understanding of how broadband pluralism and democratic politics can work together also requires attention to how fascist movements work on the visceral register of culture. For intense devotees of aspirational fascism may grasp intersections between the refined and visceral registers of public life better than some devotees of democracy and pluralism do. Is that because too many democrats foolishly act as if affective contagion flows only through authoritarian and fascist movements?

15. We note simply that von Mises, Friedman, and Hayek, all early theorists of neoliberalism, also accepted fascism at strategic moments as a way to protect a regime from either democratic socialism or Bolshevism: von Mises in Nazi Germany, Friedman in Pinochet's Chile, and, late in life, Hayek with respect to Chile.

Bodily Practices and Fascist Modes of Attunement

Fascism and Class

In a commanding book titled *Social Policy in the Third Reich: The Working Class and the National Community,* Timothy Mason explores Nazi relations to the working class during its rise to power in Germany and, to some extent, after consolidating that power. He calls manual workers a class rather than a group because they stand in a conflictual relation with the owners of capital rather than being merely one segment in a larger, organic order.

Class conflict was intense from 1918, when Germany lost the war, to 1934, when Hitler consolidated power over the regime. The conflicts between communists and social democrats, on one side, and Nazis, on the other, involved a lot of street violence, as Nazism arose during an epoch of "acute class conflict throughout Western Europe, when relations between capital and labour, left and right, were the axis of public affairs."[1] A highly organized industrial working class, indeed, posed the major mode of resistance against the rise and eventual domination of Nazism.

Mason does not argue, however, that industrial capitalists became a ruling class after the Nazi victory, with the fascists merely painting a varnish on top of class rule. He is too subtle for that. In broad agreement with Franz Neumann, he says that the capitalist industrial elite adjusted to fascism to protect its interests and that the Nazis carried out aggressive war and imperial policies as it decimated Jews, Romani, homosexuals, and labor union

1. Tim Mason, *Social Policy in the Third Reich: The Working Class and the National Community: 1918–1939* (London: Bloomsbury, 1993), 284.

leaders—in ways that wildly exceeded the necessities of capitalist maintenance. It was thus a terrible misnomer of history to allow the phrase "national socialism" to stick, because Nazism actually turned a new leaf in the rocky history of capitalist regimes.

Mason also discusses Germany's "dual state," in which the regular state bureaucracy was matched and dominated by Party organizations monitoring them.[2] He is well aware, too, of numerous Party units that paralleled and monitored urban police activity, labor groups, education, and family life, though he may fail to register closely enough the relevance of fascist drives to adjust the "social pluralism" and "social interests" of that day to the need for a new kind of pluralism today. He shows how Party controls transformed numerous constituencies into Party-controlled subsidiaries, even those these attempts did not succeed perfectly.

Hitler thought, Mason says, that his rule required him to avoid repetition of the working-class "stab in the back of 1918." It was a "stab" because, without the revolt of the working class late in the war, Hitler contends, Germany would have won. So after being appointed to office in 1933, Hitler sought to bring the labor movement under full control to avoid a second "stab in the back." Its leaders must be eliminated until this body—which would become a "rabble" without its "head"—lost that head. Only then could massive programs of labor reeducation be enacted. Part of the Mason book is devoted to the task of explaining how this agenda was resisted passively after Hitler came to rule.

In its first version, then, published in 1978, Mason interprets the working class to have been subdued by Hitler, but he concludes that it did not buy actively into the regime's aggressive imperi-

2. The phrase dual state, I believe, was coined by Max Fraenkel in *The Dual State: A Contribution to the Theory of Dictatorship* (1942; repr., Oxford: Oxford University Press, 2017). The dual state was one in which the Nazi Party organized parallel units to monitor diverse constituencies, localities, and state institutions. So rule by the Führer and rule of law became progressively fused, allowing the regime to draw on traditional norms of obedience to the law to sustain itself.

alism, intense racism, or death camps. Did Mason's counterideal of collectivism spawn gaps in his reading of the relation between Nazism and the responses of some segments of the working class to it after the Hitler takeover? Did these ideals tempt some to switch allegiance, under pressure, from an egalitarian community to a racial *Volk* community? If so, are other ideals and practices better suited to inoculating a regime against fascist temptations?

Well, when Mason returned to reappraise his own study twelve years later, he found it to have been insightful but "deeply flawed." Working-class movements had resisted Nazism, but after the defeat of its leaders in the mid-1930s and the extreme escalation of racist rhetoric, demands, and policies, a portion of that class—particularly in rural areas and small towns—did become active supporters of the movement. The Nazi drive to anti-Semitism, on Mason's first account, had been "a matter of insignificance to the German Working Class," meaning that they did not join into the movement with enthusiasm.[3] He now notes, however, how the new, aggressive "social racism" had crossed class boundaries by the mid-1930s. The "Nazi eugenics" that had vilified Jews, homosexuals, Romani, and the mentally ill, as it associated labor leaders and communists with them, also "erected a positive stereotype of the useful, worthy members of the community."[4] It was this "flattery" of good German citizens in the name of racial community—by contrast to those vehemently defined as vile, treacherous, degenerate, and scum—that Mason now says functioned as a powerful force of conversion to varying degrees across classes. Nazism now both flattered those defined to be Aryan and made them eager to avoid falling into any of the degenerate categories. That combination allowed the regime to promulgate its own "classless society": one in which true Germans could be united in racial commonality reaching across the social hierarchy. The Nazi image of a class-

3. Mason, *Social Policy,* 278.
4. Ibid., 282.

less society was designed to displace the images of collectivism advanced by social democrats and communists.

But what encouraged Mason to underplay the class transcendence of Nazism in the first version of the book, particularly since some theories of "totalitarianism" had recorded this phenomenon before his study came out? Arendt provides one example here, as Mason himself now notes in the appendix to his book. Writing in the 1950s, Arendt explores how Nazism aimed at a classless society in which the retention of hierarchy was to be transcended by "classless" identification with the racial *Volk*.

Here is what Mason says about this issue in the later appendix: "approaches and theories have their emotional foundations, and I have always remained emotionally, and thus intellectually, paralyzed about what the Nazis did and what their victims suffered."[5] This stark and honest statement could doubtless be interpreted in a few ways. Certainly it includes regret that he had not penetrated to the core of the class distribution of the social phenomenon he sought to help ward off in the future. I also sense it to manifest a belated admission of how the social ideal that consumes a thinker infiltrates into the modes of explanation offered. It may indicate, specifically, how Mason's ideal of communitarianism had inhibited him from appreciating deeply enough the multiclass attractions of Nazism once the Marxist ideal of collectivism had been defeated.

Mason belatedly acknowledges a feature of political thought to which genealogy must attend. The ideal one harbors slides into the explanatory work one does. And, sometimes, you must work on received explanatory assumptions and ideals together upon encountering unexpected events. The advent of fascism is one such event. This issue may make a difference to the work on Nazism by Neumann and Marcuse too.

A more "thorough" account of the attractions of Nazism—if there can be such a thing as a thorough account—would explore

5. Ibid.

the role that Jews as bankers, store owners, merchants, and so on, were constrained to play as the "face" an exploitative capitalism displayed to struggling workers and the middle class, the subordinate place Germany held in a European imperial system in which other states had already exploited colonies outside Europe, American participation in colonialism abroad and genocide and endocolonialism at home against Amerindians and African Americans that both brought immense suffering to both and provided testing grounds for techniques and practices later rolled into fascist regimes,[6] the rampant inflation after World War I that devastated workers in Germany, the devastations of the Great Depression, and other things yet. Others have pursued these themes effectively. Though, as Karl Polanyi reviews in *The Great Transformation,* numerous fascist movements were launched in response to the grimness of the Great Depression, and only a few succeeded.

It is important to note, additionally, how difficult it is to assess the sentiments of the working class after Hitler took power. Here is one thing Hitler himself said about the takeover of young boys who were drawn into his organizations: "These boys join our organization at the age of ten and get a breath of fresh air for the first time; then four years later, they move from the *Jungvolk* to the Hitler Youth and then we keep them for another four years. And then we are even less prepared to give them back into the hands

6. This is one of many virtues to be found in Hannah Arendt, *The Origins of Totalitarianism, Part III* (New York: Harcourt, 1968), where she reviews how imperial powers tested techniques and practices of colonial power in foreign territories eventually brought back into the imperial centers themselves. The American treatment of Amerindians provides one compelling example. The original text came out in 1951. Alex Barder, in *Empire Within: International Hierarchy and Its Imperial Laboratories* (New York: Routledge: 2015), extends this account. He shows how many techniques of power, discipline, and surveillance Foucault explores in *Discipline and Punish,* trans. Alan Sheridan (New York: Pantheon Books), were first tested in colonial hinterlands before being brought back to the home front.

of those who create our class and status barriers, rather we take them into the Party, into the Labor Front, into the SA or the SS, and so on."[7]

It is not easy, then, to assess how spontaneous, imposed, or manipulated the growth of support for Nazism was. Mason saw that. Nonetheless, this fact might encourage us to dig more deeply into dimensions Mason himself did not emphasize: the role of relational bodily disciplines in predisposing some constituencies to fascism and the possible relation between the social ideals competing for attention at one time and the susceptibility to fascism. Classical liberalism, communism, social democracy, and Nazism competed for primacy after World War I in Germany. What would have happened if multifaceted, egalitarian pluralism had been actively on the agenda? We will tap in to the question of bodily attunements in the remainder of this chapter and turn to the potential of a (corrected) pluralist ideal to counter fascist ideals of the ruthless self and the aggressive nation in chapter 3.

Group Psychology?

What encourages specific constituencies, when a situation is fraught, to embrace fascist appeals? Some theorists may respond to this question by generalizing the risk of negative affective contagion too radically. They may focus on the issue of fascist contagion, as they should, but risk losing sight of the positive modes of affective communication a democratic, pluralist culture requires to sustain itself across multiple differences. Avoidance of the essential ambiguity of affective communication, if pursued too far, can itself become tethered to austere ideals of politics. These aus-

7. Quoted in Robert O. Paxton, *The Anatomy of Fascism* (New York: Vintage Books, 2004), 143–44. This book is admirable in several ways, including for its ability to grasp how working-class support for Nazism grew, even though there continued to be more passive resistance within this class than within several others.

tere practices, in the face of historic shocks, can boomerang back to foster fascist movements. Thus drives to a politics of austerity—classical liberalism, individualism, and neoliberalism may provide diverse candidates for such a designation—can inadvertently open a window to fascist contagion when an austere program joined to the demand for mass apathy runs into a crisis it is not resilient enough to manage. Such a combination can spawn a disaffected segment of the populace vulnerable to fascist appeals during a depression, deindustrialization, or intense refugee pressures in the wake of a civil war or drought. Indeed, a pluralist ideal itself divorced from economic egalitarianism can do so too, as we shall explore in the next chapter.

Marcuse, in that early essay noted earlier, issued such a charge against the classical liberalism of his day—a mode of liberalism that looks a lot like the neoliberalism of today. He may, however, have himself responded to the dangers of mass neglect, austerity, and coldness by underestimating the signal importance democratic, egalitarian pluralism can play in both warming up life and insulating it from fascist infusions. Certainly no social ideal rises entirely above such dangers when disruptive events roll in fast. But there may well be significant differences between social ideals on this score.

Do we need a positive theory of mimetic communication that both helps to counter such dangers and opens the door to a generous ethos of engagement between multiple constituencies as it does? My sense that this is so encourages me to pass through and beyond Freud's admirable attempt to think crowd contagion in quasi-universal terms, as he, for the most part, seeks a social order that rises above the politics of affective contagion. The tight rope to walk in this domain may thus be more delicate than even Freud's balancing act suggests.

In *Group Psychology and the Ego,* published in the restless year of 1921, before the Hitler movement had become extremely powerful, Freud rehearses the impressive theory of crowd contagion advanced by Gustav Le Bon:

"The most striking peculiarity presented by a psychological group is the following: Whoever be the individuals that compose it, however like or unlike be their mode of life, their occupations, their character or their intelligence, the fact that they have been transformed into a group puts them in possession of a sort of collective mind which makes them feel, think, and act in a manner quite different from that which each individual of them would feel, think, and act were he in isolation." And as Le Bon also says, "the individual forming part of a group acquires, solely from numerical considerations a sentiment of invincible power which allows him to yield to instincts which, had he been alone, he would have perforce lost under restraint."[8]

Crowd contagion is said by Le Bon to be both a mysterious and a powerful force. Set aside for the moment how you might resist attractions at, say, a Trump, Mussolini, Hitler, Palin, or Le Pen rally. Think, first, of sports, musical, protest, religious, or comedic events to which you were mildly predisposed before you arrived and then found yourself completely carried away with crowd fervor. As I was the first time I heard the Talking Heads in a concert. Now we are talking. Such crowd formations, says Le Bon, draw out instincts that otherwise would simmer in the background. Freud, in his engagement with Le Bon, pounces on the word "instinct."

I will, to elaborate Le Bon and Freud a bit, portray an instinct to be an unconscious, purposive tendency to action that can be activated by a social trigger.[9] A young woman who looks a lot like your mother when she was young might call up something that leads you, say, to stare a trifle too long as she sits nearby. An uncanny relation between trigger, instinct, and behavior. Or simmering

8. Freud, *Group Psychology*, 7, 9.

9. The question of how instincts can be socially incorporated even if there is no master list of basic or primary instincts with significant specificity is explored in William E. Connolly, *Facing the Planetary: Entangled Humanism and the Politics of Swarming* (Durham, N.C.: Duke University Press, 2017), chapters 2 and 3. The place of creativity is addressed there too. So when we explore Theweleit's account of soldierly disciplines that foster the "armored male," it will be important to bear in mind how unconscious instincts, once incorporated, carry along with them mini modes of agency and capacities to join other instincts in creative productions.

resentment against a rising minority that challenges the historic experience of white entitlement might be intensified in a crowd setting by a leader who stokes it relentlessly with an inflammatory speech. Here the leader and crowd together amplify a shared set of anonymous instincts. But how did the instincts themselves, hovering below conscious attention, come into being? Is it time for some heavy theory lifting?

Freud thinks he has a better theory of instincts than Le Bon. The theory in this specific book, at least, locates the organization of instinctual life first in patriarchal family life and more deeply yet in the inheritance of archaic memory traces that are too fragmentary to take the shape of explicit recollections. Repression thus plays a key role in shaping instincts, in governing them, and in setting them up for release.

Some who resist Freudian theory may be tempted to relinquish the theme of unconscious instincts at this point in favor of reducing the world to the play of diverse "social interests" or, alternatively, pursuing a rational order in which collective deliberation replaces or rises above such appeals. Another route to a revision of Freud, however, is to emphasize the importance of unconscious instincts to individual and collective life, to contest his general theory of their basic origin and shape, and to explore the fraught relation between the organization of cultural dispositions and the formation of instincts. Now instincts are acknowledged to be real, but their cultural specificity depends to a significant degree upon bodily disciplines and rituals specific to a regime or constituency. Those consolidated can then be activated through affective contagion. That is pretty much the approach adopted by Klaus Theweleit, to be considered shortly. Retain instincts; reconfigure Freud's theory.

Freud contends that psychoanalytic theory is superior to both rationalist theories that underplay the potential power of instincts, crowds, and the Führer principle and to theories of crowd behavior that fail to come to terms with the generic structure of instinctive life. Le Bon, in short, poses the right issues in Freud's view, but he needs a deeper theory of the origin, role, and power of instincts.

What, then, is the group mind? Well, Freud says, "Le Bon him-self shows us by way of pointing to its similarity with the mental life of primitive people and of children."[10] We see how Freud's account already expresses an element in an imperial perspective—the purported need "primitive" peoples have to receive tutelage from more advanced countries. The general theory has already hit a stumbling block, as such generic theories often do. Freud then resists the idea that there is an intrinsic "herd instinct" that opens people to horizontal influences of affective contagion; at least he insists that such a social instinct "is at least not primary in the same sense as the instinct of self-preservation and the sexual instinct."[11] Others think that the very acquisition of desires and language draws even more fundamentally upon multiple modes of affective communication: a mother smiles at her child as she speaks; a partner cuddles it; an aunt laughs infectiously; siblings make it giggle with mimetic stunts; a neighbor speaks to it in a singsong voice, and so on. The "primary instincts," or living impetus to action, may be even more plastic than Freud tended to think.

Freud's theory of ego formation (at least in this book) is that it emerges for men out of negotiation of the Oedipal triangle. But the "successful" male remains haunted by unconscious instincts forged out of the problematic relation to the memory of the father in a patriarchal order. That can become one source of the self's hypnotic response to a "narcissistic, authoritarian" leader during a period of crisis. Such a leader must "paint in the most forcible colors, he must exaggerate, and he must repeat the same thing again and again."[12] We are thus quickly brought to the threshold at which diverse characters as Hitler, Mussolini, Le Pen, and Trump enter the scene.

We have only walked to the edge of the Freudian theory of suggestibility, even though there are already counterthreads that

10. Freud, *Group Psychology,* 13.
11. Ibid., 65.
12. Ibid., 14.

could be pulled and tugged almost against his wishes. Marcuse does the latter in *Eros and Civilization,* for instance, and so have feminist authors, such as Judith Butler, Margaret Mahler, and Victoria Pitts-Taylor.[13] But for Freud, the power of the leadership principle during a crisis is grounded in two interdependent sources: the general structure (putatively) of the patriarchal family, with its Oedipal triangle, and an archaic heritage inscribed in civilization as such in the "memory traces" of a male despot who dominated the "primal horde."

Women are not discussed as subjects, either at this point or hardly anywhere in the book under review, only as actual and potential objects. One drive of the theory is to articulate how the emergence of both horizontal connections and ego strength among men is precarious.

How, again, did the ego and horizontal connections ("group psychology") arise? "One can imagine only one possibility: the primal father had prevented his sons from satisfying directly sexual impulsions. He forced them into abstinence and consequently the emotional tie . . . ; he forced them, so to speak, into group psychology. His sexual jealousy and intolerance became in the last resort the causes of group psychology."[14] The sons forge horizontal connections out of shared rage against a despotic father who excludes them from sexual pleasure. Kill the tyrant, only to be plagued by guilt for killing the one who had also provided horde unity.

Men carry memory traces of both the Oedipal conflict and ruthless dominance of the narcissistic brute in the primal horde. Such traces are too incomplete to take the shape of explicit recollections, but when the traces resonate with fraught situations and

13. See Herbert Marcuse, *Eros and Civilization* (Boston: Beacon Press, 1955); Judith Butler, *Antigone's Claim* (New York: Columbia University Press, 2002); Victoria Pitts-Taylor, *The Brain's Body: Neuroscience and Corporeality* (Durham, N.C.: Duke University Press, 2016). Margaret Mahler, whom I have not read, is discussed extensively by Theweleit in his own revision of Freudianism.

14. Freud, *Group Psychology,* 72.

the demands of a narcissistic leader, they readily spawn aggressive crowd behavior.

I am not, by the way, wary of the idea of memory traces itself. Instincts surely find expression in such traces, and they do resonate in individuals and crowds. I am wary of this theory of how they are (and must be?) organized. I am critical of the idea that we retain memory traces of a primal horde, both because such a notion seems improbable (even though Augustine also identified primal traces of an original sin stuck in the memory bank of humans) and because it explains fascism in ways that may too severely limit the exploration of democratic options to it.[15] Freud overexplains the power of the leader, making an alternative ethos of politics that could ward off temptations of attraction to it seem rare. To him, perhaps, the best cultural agenda is to strengthen "the soft voice of reason" enunciated by an elite, whereas I suspect that such an agenda can create fascist reactions to it in the wake of a major crisis or two. The fragility of things forms a background to the theory of multifaceted democracy I embrace—particularly during the era of the Anthropocene—but receptive, horizontal modes of affective communication across diverse constituencies help to render such an ethos resilient.[16] Better, a broadband ethos

15. In *The Emotional Tie: Psychoanalysis, Mimesis, and Affect* (Palo Alto, Calif.: Stanford University Press, 1993), Mikkel Borch-Jacobsen attacks Freud's critique of hypnosis and affective communication on the grounds that it misunderstands modes of horizontal communication, overplays the logic of necessity in the fascist leadership principle, and gives too much authority to Freudian therapists to lead followers out of this mess. His examination of horizontal connections is valuable, in my view. However, he identifies Freud's theory as itself containing fascist tendencies. That is too much to take with respect to a man who had to escape the regime that enacted the Holocaust.

16. I explore these issues in *The Fragility of Things: Self-Organizing Processes, Neoliberal Fantasies, and Democratic Activism* (Durham, N.C.: Duke University Press, 20013). The focus there is on intersections between the fragility (for us) of self-organizing nonhuman processes and democratic culture. This book, I believe, resonates with an earlier one by Judith Butler,

of pluralism supported by positive interinvolvements between affective communication and ideological work is needed.

Am I expressing "resistance"? Freud does regularly introduce axioms that he knows many will resist initially, in part because they sound outlandish and in part, he thinks, because of denial of an uncanny sense they already have of them. He then supports the axioms by showing how they explain things that would otherwise remain mysterious. In this case, the axiom of the primal horde helps to explain the power of a narcissistic leader. So when he says that "even today members of a group stand in need of an illusion that they are equally and justly loved by their leader, but the leader himself need love no one else, he may be of a masterful nature, absolutely narcissistic, self-confident and independent,"[17] he is contending that this condition reveals how powerful the apparently outlandish theory of the primal horde is in fact.

A bit more ambiguity—that is a bit more appreciation of plural possibilities simmering in the generic situations characterized— appears when Freud asserts in an appendix, "But it was by love for their mothers and sisters that the mob of brothers was, as we have seen, driven to parricide. One of the reactions to the parricide after all was the institution of totemic exogamy, the prohibition of any sexual relations with the women of the family who had been tenderly loved since childhood."[18] Here, at least, you note how tender love and warm intersubjective attachments are in play prior to the two primal events recorded—the Oedipal triangle and the killing of the primal father. You may suspect that Freud's portrayal of primal events generalizes them too broadly and situates them too deeply. Freud was too impressed by the social life of great apes and insufficiently so by different processes of sexuality, child rear-

Precarious Life: The Powers of Mourning and Violence (New York: Verso, 2004). Who is deemed worthy of grieving and why is a key question informing this protean text.

17. Freud, *Group Psychology*, 71.

18. Ibid., 94.

ing, and horizontal modes of affective communication in the life of bonobos. Indeed, the latter paleontological studies were probably not yet available to him. Females have far more power, autonomy, and standing in the latter kind of regime. No patriarchal male dominates all erotic pleasures or governs all intimate ties.

The putative strength of Freud's theory of instincts and mass suggestibility resides in its ability to explain how the process of ego formation is haunted by instinctive attractions to a narcissistic leader. The weakness of the theory resides in its overdetermination. That is, in generalizing the processes under review, Freud may understate how many resist such attractions and how alternative modes of child rearing; the breadth, blending, and diversity of kinship ties; education; modes of work; gender relations; sexual relations; political participation; and military life play in forming relational selves, in opening them to modes of affective communication, and in insulating them from mimesis grounded in narcissistic leadership. The tendency of the theory—though we have noted at least one countertendency—is to disavow the positive power of affective communication because the silo theory it supports renders us primarily alert to its dangerous potential. It thus seems wise to consult another perspective that both addresses the power of fascist contagion under harsh circumstances and suggests a route to alternative modes of association and affective communication.

With those who say that Freud does deal with these social issues adequately elsewhere I will not dissent too vociferously. But I would want that claim to be assessed against the reading in what follows of how specific bodily practices help both to organize the shape of instincts and to define specific attunements to affective contagion.

The Selectively Armored Body

In *The Civilizing Process,* Norbert Elias reviews a series of historical shifts in normative bodily practices that arose among privileged classes in Europe between 1300 and 1800. During the early period, polite people were told not to throw gnawed bones back onto the table but, rather, behind them on the floor; loud farting in public settings, it was said, was impolite and would make others compare you to an animal or peasant; strange men who found themselves sleeping together in the same bed at an inn were advised not to talk too much before falling asleep; dinner napkins, it was said, were not to be used for blowing your nose during the common meal.

A list of bodily norms that seems crude to us joined to a blunt set of comparisons to peasants and animals. It was not as if there were no norms, then. Indeed, men and women who were too fastidious in their dinner habits, dressing gown practices, control of belches and passing wind, refusals to share a bed at an inn, and so on, could be subject to ridicule. But the norms wired into bodily practices did not enact as strong separations between public and private, self and other, humans and nature, bodily display and inner bodily organization, as those practiced later. For example, the later introduction of knives, forks, and individual plates for dining separated eating from other aspects of nature more than had eating at a common table, and so did the subtraction of the entire animal from the feast table and the introduction of distanced, polite terms such as pork and beef to describe meat rather than naming directly the animal from which it had been wrested.

Freud's theory of instinctive organization, from the Elias point of view, rests more upon a set of modern, European normative bodily relations than he had appreciated. That theory might not work so well for bodily practices and social instincts organized in the rustic Europe of 1300.[19] To put it another way, the organic impetus to desire promulgated by Elias is more plastic in its potentialities than that posited by Freud's theory of primary instincts and

19. See Norbert Elias, *The Civilizing Process,* vol. 1, trans. Edmund Jephcott (New York: Urizen Books, 1978).

generic family relations. Hence he must pay closer attention to historical shifts in the organization of instincts. In *Male Fantasies,* a two volume text first published in Germany in 1978, Klaus Theweleit professes a debt to Norbert Elias, as well as to Gilles Deleuze and Félix Guattari, Michel Foucault, and Luce Irigaray. He examines bodily disciplines and rituals that attracted men to fascist movements in Germany of the 1920s in particular, both predisposing them to violent acts on behalf of a racialized *Volk* and priming them to receive shots of adrenaline from the Führer in the making. The bodily disciplines of a select group of soldiers do carry them to a place rather close to that Freud had grasped through failures of the Oedipal complex and the inheritance of primal traces from horde life. And Freud had devoted a brief chapter to the organization of the Catholic Church and armies to illustrate his theory of identification with the leader. But the route Theweleit traces is more invested with specific bodily practices and rituals than Freud had emphasized. It focuses on the variable relations between specific modes of bodily discipline and the emergence of instincts. It explores how fascist dispositions to ruthlessness are formed.

We can anticipate the study Theweleit attempts through his review of the organization of one aristocratic ballet in the early modern period. Yes, the choreography of the ballet in question represents the subordination of aristocratic women to the king, the eroticization of these women to men lower on the hierarchy who find them to be unavailable, the domination of men over women in each class, and the domination of human beings over the earth, itself represented to be feminine—an ideology represented in the roles and rhythms of a dance.

Yes, yes, yes. But more is involved, too. The tight choreography of male and female bodies enacts an intensive, rhythmic organization of muscles, movements, brain activities, eye contacts, and hormonal secretions that fold specific relations of authority, exoticization, and subordination into bodily habits, instincts, and routines of desire.[20] The dance choreography induces "streams of desire" that exceed the powers of representation.[21]

Viewers, too, do not merely watch the representations. Simulations of these bodily movements are folded, if prior susceptibility to them is operative, into the bodily practices and modes of relational attunement of viewers during the performance. To see is to touch and be touched, as we note more definitely when we recall that the eye evolved out of an organ of touch and still retains traces of that capacity. Think of the haptic image organized, for instance, when the skin of a vibrant young dancer is conveyed to viewers, who invoke tacit memories of having caressed supple skin in the past. The recent discovery of mirror neurons in the 1990s reenforces Theweleit's account of the injection of ballet choreography into the sensorium and instinctive tendencies to action of enchanted viewers. The effects are hypnotic.

Our gaits, hormonal secretions, rhythms of conduct, tacit rules of eye contact, facial habits of expression, skin dilation or tightening, memory layered modes of perception, and relational presumptions convey such disciplines into habitual modes of response. The socialization of instincts. The young girl in a 1950s movie looks down demurely when she encounters a man of power and authority. So does the throwback virgin in *Fifty Shades of Grey* (2015), lightly biting her lower lip as she summons the courage to ask the imposing young tycoon hovering over her demanding questions during the first interview. His bodily responses anticipate embraces that could arrive later. So does the coterie of young women who take messages and usher visitors into his suite with its sweeping views of the city.

20. For a thoughtful study of how other styles of dancing both express relational generosity and fold such dispositions into the habitus of the dancers, see Erin Manning, *Always More Than One: Individuation's Dance* (Durham, N.C.: Duke University Press, 2013).

21. Klaus Theweleit, *Male Fantasies,* vol. 1, *Women, Floods, Bodies, History,* trans. Stephen Conway (Minneapolis: University of Minnesota Press, 1987), 317.

The viewer notes the sexual tension, of course, but one may be less attentive initially to how a neoliberal choreography slides effortlessly into the demeanor and expectations of viewers who had not previously built up resistance to it. The latter film, in particular, conveys an exciting neoliberal economy based upon the conquest of nature, hubristic male agents riding its crest, incredible rewards available to risky investments, public applause for acts of philanthropy by the rich, university administrations buying into the larger system to cultivate a donor class, women teased into subordinate roles to enjoy such privileges, and barely noted class divisions between movers and shakers at the top of the high-rise buildings and those stuck on the lower reaches of that hierarchy.

Fifty Shades of Grey is *The Fountainhead* sexed up and adjusted modestly to a new age. Its economy of burdens and entitlements is curated through a choreography of movements, looks, presumptions of authority, risk, and desire more than through ideological articulation. The sexual tension concentrates the focus on one issue, as the scenes tacitly convey neoliberal attitudes and expectations about the structure of the economy.

The male tycoon and philanthropist does show signs of vulnerability; those signs are to be absorbed into womanly sympathy for the tough features in his background, as you help him bolster his rule over several spheres of life. The burdens of a class society in a neoliberal culture never come up for review, unless you wonder about that driver and those assistants, the workers who made the building, the tycoon's twelve cars, and the urban noise distributed to commoners when he hovers over the city in his helicopter. "Will she accept sexual bondage or not?" becomes the overt question as an entire image of social life slides effortlessly into bodily modes of attunement.

When I was nineteen years old, working as athletic director at a summer music camp in Northern Michigan, several counselors from a big college football program and I hung out together. I had played football in high school, replete with its rituals, authority routines, modes of bodily attunement, specific athletic skills, and bouts of ribald humor; they were still immersed in intense versions of them. One day, a camp musician and intellectual whom I admired pulled me aside to say, "They may have to walk that way, but you don't; it is at odds with the rest of your being." After in turn blushing, getting irritated at the intrusion, and beginning to think, I checked out the unconscious rhythm of that stride. It was assertive: "I'm a nice guy, but don't mess with me too much." It was also wired in from a few years of imitating the strides of older players. Gradually, I reworked that gait some, doing so to alter my self-presentation a bit as well as to adjust the mode of self-organization embedded in it. A minor change, no doubt, almost nothing. But it did convey to me an initial sense of the intimate intersections between bodily ritual, self-performance, instinct formation, and relational expectations. Since college and professional football today provides one of the sites at which neofascist practices are rehearsed and observed in America, as images of military aggression and competitive sports form an almost seamless intertext, the example is perhaps not altogether trivial. Walk the way you seek to think and feel; allow new thoughts bubbling up to find expression in the style of your gait, the tone of your voice, and the tilt of your head. It is the work back and forth between bodily demeanor, thinking, and articulations that counts.

Theweleit is interested in the bodily drills and behavioral demands of soldierly German males, from just after the defeat of Germany in World War I through the consolidation of German Nazism. Many of the former organized the *Freikorps,* the "free" soldiers who provided the violent cutting edge of the Nazi movement in its violent street fights with social democrats and communists for rule during the difficult days of the Weimar Republic.

Examining novels and diaries written by several soldiers returning from defeat, he found a strange vacuity in their talk about wives and other women. The woman was not to be named but to be grasped in subordinate, functional roles as mother and wife. Other women were often defined as sluts and whores, sometimes to be used in a predatory, violent way, more often to be defined as "scum" to express contempt and, above all, the fear of giving into the viscous, fluid elements not entirely dried out in the interior of the soldier male. These insistent representations of women reflected the bodily organization of the soldierly male. The drills, battles, and experience of devastating wartime defeat combined to shape and define soldierly males as machines of vengeance and ruthlessness.

The military cadet enters an academy with a strict, aggressive hierarchy. He is instructed to obey the whims of those above him and to exercise whimsical control over those below. Refusal of either assignment brings physical punishment: beatings, demands to carry out arduous exercises to the point of exhaustion, and so on. The whimsical character of the orders prepares the cadet instinctively to accept blind obedience. "The cadet never receives instructions; he recognizes his mistakes only in the moment of transgression from the reactions of others who already know the score . . . ; each newcomer thus necessarily repeats the mistakes of his predecessors, who in turn recognize and welcome the apparent opportunity to treat their successors as they themselves have previously been treated."[22] In drilling for combat, the body is repeatedly pushed to exhaustion amid the demand that it continue past that point. Organized ruthlessness toward oneself and selected others becomes the order of the day. Punishment often takes the form of doing woman's work, to underline how puny the punished one is and how subordinate women must be in a militaristic world. "And little by little the body accepts these painful interventions. . . . It receives them as experiences of satisfaction."[23]

Eventually the successful cadet finds "any kind of solicitous care quite intolerable."[24] The element of softness and fluidity,

22. Klaus Theweleit, *Male Fantasies,* vol. 2, *Male Bodies, Psychoanalyzing the White Terror,* trans. Erica Carter and Chris Turner (Minneapolis: University of Minnesota Press, 1988), 145.

23. Ibid., 2:150.

24. Ibid., 2:151.

which many had experienced as boys with mothers and friends, is drilled out of them. But not entirely eliminated. The "woman" inside now becomes an anxiety leaders tap as they transfigure the embodied fear of feminine fluids into the production of a machine of male aggression in the service of the lieutenant, the nation as racial *Volk,* and the Führer—all communicated through concentric spirals of mimetic authority. One man, one troop, one harsh rhythm of action, one Führer. The troop produces "an expression of battle and of a specific masculinity."[25] This is an alpha masculinity hungry for violence against external and internal foes of the *Volk*; it is primed to be inspired by affective dictates from military leaders and the Führer.

When Hitler, in a scene many have seen, takes off his hat to walk between two lines of tightly assembled troops who have been inspired by him for an hour or two, he is in effect fucking the troops in the aggressive style they must themselves adopt with respect to their targets of vilification. Be raped to do rape, either to women or to other constituencies said to be inhabited by the lascivious characteristics lurking in "woman."

Hardness, ruthlessness, and obedience to arbitrary authority are the orders of the day; these instincts now become set in the cast of the male jaw; the rigidity of his stance; the sharp salutes repeated endlessly; the visceral agitations set off by a bloodred flag and black swastika; the tightness in the back of the neck; the determined gait; the butt of a gun ready to bring down on Jews, commies, homosexuals, or social democrats; the shouts of "Heil!"; and a variety of other bodily prompts that link merciless behavior against the enemy to resistance against indispensable remnants of softness, vulnerability, or care circulating in the self. These are the "molecular intruders who must be dispensed with."[26] Better, perhaps, these are remnants that must not be destroyed entirely

25. Ibid., 2:155.
26. Ibid., 2:183.

in soldier males so that they can be first tapped and then funneled into militant obedience to the Führer.

Perhaps this is a pertinent place to note a near-paradox: a con-centrically ordered culture deeply engrained with obedience to law—the rule of law—can, under conditions of stress, become transfigured into a culture in which regular people become too adjusted to the law of rule. Under conditions of stress, habits of untrammeled obedience can be transmitted from one domain to the other. As we shall see, one of the virtues of multifaceted de-mocracy is that it contains productive tensions that work against such transfigurations.

It must be emphasized in ways that Theweleit does not always do that these drills and disciplines help to generate preliminary tendencies to purposive action, not iron determinants. One set of trained, engrained, instinctive purposes might be qualified by others; those bearing them may also encounter more refined judg-ments that inhibit, encourage, or amplify them. The drills, bodi-ly demeanors and group pressures make a difference but do not settle everything. For example, drives to violence might encoun-ter opposing feelings, propelling a soldier down a suicidal path, as happens often enough. Or, once you escape that regimenta-tion, you may work tactically on some of those bodily instincts, doing so to modify a few of your own tendencies to action. That is why Michel Foucault, for instance, made so much of "tactics of the self," bodily tactics by which you work upon some engrained tendencies to loosen or alter them. Anyway, the tendencies them-selves vary in the degrees of ambivalence and definition in them among people subjected to the same drills, as they become synthe-sized unconsciously in relation to clusters already there. Instincts as purposive tendencies.

One way to emphasize this point is to say that those who have been injected with the disciplines of armored males may find such tendencies (instincts) ignited through crowd contagion when they encounter a leader with the rhetorical brilliance of Hitler, whose adult life was devoted to pulling such tendencies in one direction rather than others. Hitler's rhetorical powers were aided by such bodily practices, and the practices spurred crowds to new heights of response. The speeches and training resonated together. Hitler rehearsed often and carefully to devise specific bodily gestures apt to solicit the most intense crowd reactions.

I am reviewing this study of male fantasies during the Hitler era as I write in Weimar, Germany, in summer 2017. Weimar is a beautiful, cosmopolitan and artistic town today; it also once spawned huge crowds in the main *Platz* on more than twenty occasions as Hitler delivered magnetic speeches to open wounds and ignite the faithful while standing on the balcony of the Elephant Hotel. I recently ate at that hotel. Perhaps the throngs were magnetized by speeches such as the following, delivered at the Sixth Party Conference. It may make sense to simulate the rhythms, intonations, and exclamations as you read to better feel the punches delivered during this speech:

> And because the German nation has made a proud assessment of its racial values, and with courage and daring has demanded a leadership for the Reich and the people, more and more of the people have joined this leadership and placed themselves at its service [Heil!]. . . . A nation is never made up exclusively of its truly active fighters. Thus greater demands will be made of them than of the millions of their national comrades. . . . They must take the oath, "I shall fight!" [Heil!] . . . Its doctrine will not change, its organization will be as hard as steel, its tactics will be supple and adaptable, and in its entirety it will be like a holy order [Heil, Sieg Heil, Sieg Heil!].[27]

Those men of steel rivet the fantasy of the alpha male to the steel of an aggressive nation as a holy order. The spirituality of fascism.

The "armored male," in the ideal case, has now become simultaneously an attacking machine and a funnel into which flows the contagion of fascism. Horizontal influences magnify those connections. But presumptive receptivity to horizontal bonds of care for diversity, to the extent the regime succeeds, are knocked out

27. Ibid., 2:414–15.

of the hormonal secretions of armored males. Those who express vulnerability and softness are placed under suspicion. For the nation as *Volk* is "the opposite of mass, femininity, equality, sensuous pleasure, desire and revolution."[28] That is why republican defenses of the nation as a mere regime of constitutional procedures are more apt to enrage soldierly males than to attract them; such articulations devalue and demean the virile entity the latter fantasize.

We may now glimpse a bit more closely how pursuit of either a benign nation or egalitarian collectivity at odds with multifaceted pluralism can be vulnerable, under conditions of stress, to a hostile fascist takeover. Devotees of the nation pursue a concentric world in which a series of ascending circles acquires the shape of an expanding cone, so that circular commonalities of family, locality, region, nation, and Western civilization resonate back and forth to forge a benign unity engraining people with the virtue of obedience to each circle and to the whole.[29] Fascist movements

28. Ibid., 2:277.

29. It is rather easy to see how a concentric image of the nation is susceptible to a hostile takeover. What about egalitarian communism? One problem here is that this ideal is stated so often in vague and generic terms, as can be seen in the dialogue between Alain Badiou and Peter Engelmann in *Philosophy and the Idea of Communism* (Cambridge: Polity Press, 2013). In response to Engelmann's skeptical questioning—he had been imprisoned in a Stasi camp—Badiou is vague. He projects a horizon of community and equality with no historical references, except for a whisper of connection to the Paris Commune before its defeat. But the latter was local, and the communist projection is extremely broad in it territorial coverage. The generic suspicion by Badiou of institutional mediations, a politics of pluralization, and a broadband ethos of pluralist engagements is at issue here. Is the media to be protected from the regime? Are a plurality of identities and interests projected? How do they relate? Without the latter mediations, a communist movement is susceptible to a hostile fascist takeover during a period of stress; with them, the need for institutional specification becomes imperative. Badiou rejects historical comparisons to the Soviet Union, for example, because it did not pursue a pure enough ideal. Many neoliberals do the same thing when their practices are treated by others as the sources of depression and of fascist temptations. Multifaceted democracy, by contrast to the collectivist horizon of Badiou, poses a regulative ideal replete with mediations, tensions, and resiliencies.

seek to transfigure or invert such a quest into a highly aggressive formation of authoritarian unity, with fervent families, localities, and regions funneled into a bellicose Party and the Party funneled into a Führer as the consummate figure to whom total obedience is owed. Fascists seek a hostile takeover of either national unity or a unified collectivity. Each ideal, during a time of duress, might make it more difficult to avoid such a takeover. Multifaceted democracy is less amenable to such a takeover, with its assemblage of diverse constituencies, its diverse satisfactions available to each, its multiple institutions with different degrees of autonomy, its qualifications of concentric culture, its active ambivalence toward obedience, and the affirmative ethos of engagement it negotiates across constituencies and within institutions.

A closely related point is that during a crisis, the fascist Right is typically more brutal and relentless than the Left, certainly than the democratic Left. This was proven during early Nazi offensives against opponents when the outcome was still uncertain. This drive to brutality is due in part to the harsh bodily drills and disciplines injected into fascist males. That relationship, in turn, teaches us why a culture of multifaceted democracy must find expression in both the bodily disciplines and public articulations of many so that an ethos of presumptive generosity and care across multiple differences is sustained. Such virtues must be pursued before fascism becomes consolidated, because it may be too late after its consolidation.

That may mean, too, that when a fascist movement does arise, the most promising way to respond is to form a militant pluralist assemblage to oppose it, working upon affinities of spirituality across creed, social position, age cohort, region, and identity to consolidate the assemblage it. A pluralist assemblage is not highly susceptible to a takeover, and it is well equipped to resist attempts at one, in part because it does not assume the circular form so amenable to a takeover. Pluralist modes of resilience, however, work poorly if sharp economic inequalities push some constituencies out of the assemblage. It is this last condition that devotees of pluralism themselves do not always appreciate sufficiently. We will address these features of multifaceted democracy in the next chapter.

Back to the armored males, because they can provide such important catalysts to a fascist takeover. The tendency to ruthlessness of armored males finds additional expression in terse phrase clusters such as "that is settled then, problem solved, anyone else?"[30] Such phrase clusters function as aggressive verbal shorthand, because the highest mode of communication of a fascist is violence—as in the self-report in which a soldier said, "I made it clear with my fists that we were now in absolute agreement."[31]

Those jarring phrase clusters simulate the dogmatism and violence they seek to consolidate. They may also help those outside the circle to understand the attraction of such clusters to adamant supporters of a leader like Donald Trump, including the raucous celebrations erupting at Trump rallies when a protester is roughly ushered out. "Aren't my rallies fun!" Trump loves to blurt at such moments. In aspirational fascism, definitive assertion takes priority over extended justification. Anyone who has been under the province of a tough football coach, rigid teacher, sadistic drill sergeant, authoritarian boss, or punitive parent knows that.

Of course, the production of armored bodies does not suffice to produce fascism. But to the extent such types are sprinkled to varying degrees among several constituencies, devastating events and aspirational leaders can get a fascist movement rolling. That is why it is probably not the best idea to look at only one set of large historical circumstances that have fostered powerful fascist movements in the past to see if they are in operation today. After all, the first occurrences of fascism were unique in history. In Germany in the late 1920s, Marxists both expected an economic crisis to arise—when others did not—and anticipated

30. Theweleit, *Male Fantasies,* 2:272.
31. Ibid., 2:293.

that the structural position of the working class in the capitalist system meant that communism would triumph after the crisis hit. They were correct on one count and wrong on the other, partly because fascism was a new thing and partly because the theory tethered the working class to a structural theory of political determinations. Theweleit loosens readings of structural determinations as he probes volatile intersections between bodies, movements, and politics. Politics is seldom reducible entirely to the structural setting in which it occurs.

Theweleit thus acknowledges that his bodily genealogy of one set of extreme soldierly practices does not explain why so many others were so responsive to the fascist mix of implacable rhetoric and street violence at a key juncture—and it must not be forgotten that only a large minority embraced the movement until after the Nazi takeover. But he "hypothesizes" that less radical modes of discipline sprinkled in families, schools, factories, gendered relations of desire, and the Lutheran Church of the day made notable contributions to fascist contagion. He thanks his father, a nice man and a fascist, for the harsh beatings delivered to him as a boy that helped him to feel how fascist temptations work and later encouraged him to dissect the bodily practices that encourage the attractions. I suppose I should thank my football coach, the parents of friends who regularly dispatched harsh punishments to them, and the gentleman who advised me to work upon that teenaged gait. Those earnest evangelicals who pressed so relentlessly to push me to accept conversion at a church camp when I was twelve years old deserve a bit of thanks, too.

Large events that incite distress and disturbance may vary historically in tone and severity, with rapid climate change providing one implacable force today that was not even operative as a recognized force by sociocentrists of any type in the 1930s. But the types of bodily discipline in play make a difference too. The complex conjunctions between leaders, historical disappointments, shocking events, constituency affiliations, and selective bodily dispositions may or may not coalesce into a successful fascist movement at a pivotal historical moment. There is an element of real uncertainty here. But to the extent we grasp the role of bodily practices in promoting visceral attunement to fascist rhetoric and violence during times of distress, we may be in a better position to devise counterstrategies.

It could be pertinent to punctuate this reading of bodily disciplines and fascist attunements with another mode of contagion. I have in mind the contagion that periodically sweeps financial markets and the oblique relations "contrarians" assume to that contagion. What is their bodily demeanor, and what differences and affinities inform their relations to the investing crowd, by comparison to the combinations explored earlier?[32] I defer that study, however, to move to questions about possible affinities across difference between the forces Theweleit identifies and those operative in America today.

The American Milieu

In 1950, shortly after the Allied defeat of Germany, Italy, and Japan in World War II, a new study called *The Authoritarian Personality* appeared. This study was set in America rather than in one of the defeated fascist regimes. Émigré Jewish intellectuals from Germany played a large role in the study, so one can be confident that it was done in a context of a concern to avoid here the outcome they had experienced there. One of its authors was Theodor Adorno, who later became well known in the United States as a critical theorist. We will attend in particular to his findings. The book was widely criticized by behavioral social scientists at the time for its failure to conform to the dictates of a vision of scientific method they themselves had recently inter-

32. For one illuminating study, see Urs Staheli, "Market Crowds," in *Crowds,* ed. Jeffrey Schnapp and Matthew Tiew, 271–87 (Stanford, Calif.: Stanford University Press, 2006). Several other essays in that volume speak to our topic too.

nalized. Its "Questionnaire," for instance, was thought not to be transferrable across cultures in some cases and too suggestive to those taking it in others. I will bypass those criticisms, because I take the first to set an impossible standard (yes, you might replace "Jews" with "Muslims" in several questions today, but that points to the role that affinities across differences play in the study of cultural life), and the second poses risks that the authors themselves took into account.

The study appeared during a period of rising hubris in the behavioral sciences about their capacity to explain and predict. I also bypass for the moment the prejudicial instincts toward homosexuality, African Americans, and women that unconsciously infiltrated the study itself. It was written before a set of feminist, civil rights, and gay rights movements transformed conventional attitudes through multifaceted political actions.

Adorno identifies several personality types distributed unevenly across classes and genders, even if dominant clusters are discernible. Some types were resistant to fascism—they are sometimes called the liberal or democratic types. Other types could provide potential degrees of support for a fascist movement should one arrive. And, indeed, the neofascist McCarthy movement was waiting in the wings to take a heavy toll on radical workers, labor unions, the film industry, the U.S. Congress, and the academy when the book appeared. Attitudes toward Jews and "Negroes" by whites were reviewed. The book, unfortunately, does not focus on corollary bodily practices.

The first "type," the "conventionally prejudiced," could be drawn into a fascist movement, but they also possess potential to be pulled in other directions. The second and third types exhibit more serious dangers. The authoritarian personality is rigid, prone to exert severe control over those below it to prop up its own self-confidence and highly predisposed to obey authority figures above it who demand strict loyalty and obedience. The authoritarian type identifies itself to be highly moral, but that morality is "punitive and projective." Its morality vents "fury upon whatever object is available and not too likely to strike back."[33]

The third type, the "manipulative" type, stands rather close to Freud's narcissistic leader. Indeed, the type offers a textbook anticipation of Donald Trump and several other extremist leaders. The manipulative type demands a leadership position and "avoids psychosis by reducing outer reality to a mere object of action. Thus he is incapable of positive cathexis."[34] Authoritarian types are often drawn to manipulative types through "upward identification." The latter are thus more dangerous the more authoritarian types there are around. Manipulative types enact "a kind of compulsive over-realism which treats everything and everyone as an object to be handled, manipulated, seized by the subject's own theoretical and practical concerns."[35] Loyalty, to them, is both a key virtue and a one-way street. Himmler was held to exemplify this type. And it also reminds one of some of the soldier males whose bodily regimes Theweleit examined so closely.

The study found that after the San Quentin prisoners, who had also received the "Questionnaire," members of the working class in the United States exhibited most traits of authoritarianism. It is important to emphasize, however, that while a significant minority in this class displayed such characteristics, innumerable others did not. This points to a need to find ways to encourage the latter to resist the influence of the former. There are also differences of degree here that may not have been emphasized enough in the study.

To simply call upon either very authoritarian or manipulative types to be "more caring" is apt to backfire according to this study, perhaps because the first group does not experience a hell of a lot of public care coming its way and the second is by bodily attunement viscerally hostile to an ethos of presumptive generosity across dif-

33. Theodore Adorno et al., *The Authoritarian Personality* (New York: W. W. Norton, 1950), 233.

34. Ibid., 751.

35. Ibid., 767.

ference. The latter feelings of warmth and care express feminine traits it is organized to chide in others and repress in itself at all costs. Its own traits are predatory, manipulative, and ruthless.

You can see how the Adorno study and the Theweleit account of fascist bodily disciplines could be brought to bear upon each other. Theweleit explores bodily practices that help to foster the authoritarian and manipulative types.

Another element *The Authoritarian Personality* brings out must also be emphasized. Though class and gender tendencies are discernible in its account, there is a wild card that must be acknowledged. Existential orientations to abstract revenge that attract people toward such movements can be forged out of several kinds of experience: a calamity, failure at work, social isolation, the defeat of a social movement, the decline of a state, or the intense sense of being neglected or downgraded for other reasons can draw people from a variety of social positions into affiliation with a fascist movement once the latter has become mobilized and refined its tactics of recruitment. So the class tendencies and bodily disciplines at work here must not be allowed to underplay the multiclass potential of such movements under circumstances of historical stress that breed existential resentment.

We review first, however, two constituencies in America that have already tasted severe fascist tactics and controls. Indigenous peoples first faced white genocidal drives in the nineteenth century and many were forced onto "reservations" where repeated defeats ended in treaties to be broken again. This history of conquest deserves to be studied closely.[36] As Hannah Arendt and others have

36. See, in particular, William Apess, *On Our Own Ground,* ed. Barry O'Connell (Amherst: University of Massachusetts Press, 1992), in which this early-nineteenth-century Pequot author—who is perhaps the first Amerindian to write in English—confronts nineteenth-century white Christians in "New England" who treat his people as inferiors to be converted or conquered. I examine that text in chapter 6 of *An Ethos of Pluralization* and explore how the legacy of the American conquest poses severe dilemmas for pluralizing drives today. For an excellent study

explored, some of the practices of control and repression imposed upon them in the nineteenth century were first exported to other colonial zones and later carried back to fascist states themselves. One of Donald Trump's heroes, President Andrew Jackson, encouraged vigilantes in the 1830s to disobey a U.S. Supreme Court order to recognize Cherokee rights to the land they occupied in southeastern America, until the Cherokee were forced to take a long, painful trek to Oklahoma. Donald Trump's recent actions at Standing Rock continue the Andrew Jackson tradition. They reveal how the demand to treat nature only as a field of conquest can so easily become attached to the demand to treat vilified peoples as objects of conquest. The dispositions to conquest and ruthlessness are fungible.

In *White Rage: The Unspoken Truth of Our Racial Divide,* Carol Anderson provides succinct summaries of disparate periods of white rage against blacks in America, from the period of racial chattel enslavement to the present. The term rage is revealing because it points to threatened entitlements, dreams, bodily practices, and binds that help to foster the destructive dispositions.

After the end of the Civil War, itself marked by heated white race riots against the war in New York City, short periods of promising progress by African Americans were persistently stalked by others when white rage again acquired the upper hand. This includes the dismantling of the Reconstruction through the introduction of Jim Crow and innumerable lynchings of young black men. The tactics also involved the use of "Black Codes to derail the very market forces" President Andrew Johnson purported to celebrate at the end of the war.[37] Formal celebrations of market forces by carriers of white rage are often accompanied by use of antimar-

---

of how endo-colonialism has "blown back" into fascist movements, see Alexander Barder, *Empire Within: International Hierarchy and Its Imperial Laboratories of Governance* (New York: Routledge, 2015).

37. Carol Anderson, *White Rage: The Unspoken Truth of Our Racial Divide* (New York: Bloomsbury, 2016), 26.

ket pressures, laws, and illegal acts to maintain racial hegemony, as they were by Andrew Johnson. There were also the radical legal retreats from Reconstruction by the U.S. Supreme Court. That is why the neoliberal rhetoric of the last few decades functions largely as a cover story for white triumphalism.

Another instance of violent retrenchment occurred in the 1920s, when the Great Migration north of blacks to take up new factory jobs and educational opportunities was subjected to extreme legal and illegal strategies to slow the exodus of cheap labor upon which the South depended. The creative tactics enacted to resist these efforts were impressive, but the attempts themselves both expressed southern white insistence on keeping blacks in subordinate roles and helped establish precedents and techniques northern states applied against the same constituencies. These soon arose in cities like Chicago and Detroit, where redlining, ruthless police practices, and systemic discrimination in education became rampant. Even the election of Barack Obama in 2008, expected by many (including me) to improve race relations, exacerbated white rage in several sectors of life.

Even such a brief review discloses how fascist disciplines, surveillances, and terror have been applied to Amerindians and African Americans in the United States for a very long time. In different ways and degrees, women, Jews, Italians, and homosexuals can be added to this list. The effects upon African American and Amerindian life, however, have been particularly severe and long lasting; such drives can become intensified when white constituencies sense that the "American Dream" that sustains them is in trouble and perceive no viable counterideal on the horizon.

Let's also focus for a moment on what effects the exercise of such modes of discipline, ruthlessness, and terror against minorities has on those assigned to carry them out, such as many working-class whites threatened by a loss of marginal entitlements, police officers in urban areas, prison guards, white realtors and housing association members, military personnel returning home from imperial wars, and white judicial and elected officials in states with intense traditions of racism. Those delivering these repressive practices—though there are exceptions—are apt to become hardened by the very training, ethos, and harsh practices deployed to hold the line. What you often get, to different degrees depending upon the situation, is the hardening of previously cultivated innocence—what Adorno would have called the conversion of conventional prejudice into active racism. White rage. Theweleit would understand.

White workers come to feel caught in a squeeze: from one side they are threatened by neoliberal elites who support unfettered banking practices, free trade, grotesque concentrations of wealth, and an infrastructure of consumption that makes it hard to make ends meet, as they are rendered more insecure by deindustrialization, harsh labor practices, authoritarian bosses, and severe bankruptcy rules; from another side, they feel underrepresented by noble pluralizing movements in the zones of race, sexuality, gender, and religion. A powder keg is thus waiting to be ignited. The rather harsh bodily practices to which they are often subjected at home, in the military, and at work can join with resentments about the marginal entitlements to which they cling to exacerbate the pursuit of abstract revenge.

The tone and mood engendered recall at least something of the ethos of vengeance pursued by returning soldiers in Germany after World War I. Indeed, working-class Americans who have returned from the imperial wars of Vietnam, Afghanistan, Iraq, and Syria first face harsh discipline in preparation for war, often undergo injuries and traumatic stress at the front, and then experience a strange sense of neglect and disaffection upon returning home. Who wants to celebrate returnees from ill-considered conflicts (except Donald Trump, of course, who seeks to pull those grievances in one direction)?

With few elites and activists to focus on your struggles and tribulations, your jaw becomes set, your neck muscles tighten, and you place yourself on high alert to note any insult or oversight tossed casually in your direction. You react intensely to small slights. Think of those white veterans carefully placed behind Donald Trump at his rallies. The tense bodies they once had have slackened, but the fierceness of those implacable faces has grown more severe. Such implacable refugees from mistaken, devastating wars readily become susceptible to narcissistic leaders who speak in abrupt sentences; identify convenient enemies; utter Big Lies upon which to hang grievances; and purport to grasp their needs, feelings, and interests. I would like to thank a few blue-collar white men in the neighborhoods of my youth for helping me to recognize such tendencies. The numerous noble resisters deserve high respect too.

Private white militia in the American Midwest and Far West exhibit an extreme version of such dispositions. They organize bodily disciplines and military routines to prepare for a day of reckoning. Guns play a key role in their identities and the priorities they carry with them into families, bars, workplaces, churches, Facebook trolling, and neighborhoods. Some have already participated in violent events. And tendencies toward vigilante violence are on the rise.

One day several years ago, my partner and I were riding bikes in the thumb area of Michigan. I had been paying attention to militia organizations springing up here and there after a militia attack. We rode down a deserted road and bumped into a large rural housing enclave. The entrance was framed by a huge green tractor on one side of a startlingly high flag pole with a huge American flag at its top and a large red tractor gracing the other side. Let's just ride casually through this neighborhood, the two amateur ethnographers decided. It's a free country. Within five minutes, a large black pickup truck was tailing us. We speeded up a bit, and it speeded up with us. Then, facing strictly to the front as we spoke to each other through clenched jaws, we decided to set a steady pace until we could wind our way out of that labyrinth and back onto the country road. Luckily the truck stopped when we turned right to head down the deserted road at a carefully measured pace, leaving the tractors, American flag, housing enclave, and truck behind. We had no secondary plan if it had turned to follow us down that desolate road. We were received as white enemies of the white militia. "Make America Great Again."

We noted in the discussion of "armored males" in pre-Nazi Germany how repetitive, draconian discipline can instill aggressive instincts without controlling their exact direction of expression. Many working-class people in America today are refugees from a series of destructive wars. For those of us who have escaped such trials because the draft has been eliminated, Stanley Kubrick's 1987 film *Full Metal Jacket* provides an insightful account of how such military practices approach the drills and conditions explored by Theweleit. Set in 1968, it first portrays the rigors of a marine boot camp on Parris Island—an infamous place of training—and then places the survivors in Vietnam to face the Tet Offensive of 1968. Kubrick digs down to show how the drills are designed to turn marines into killing machines as the recruits seek to evade the drill sergeant's constant designations of them as "ladies" and "maggots." Here is one chant repeated rhythmically as trainees trot alongside the drill sergeant: "I don't know but I've been told, Eskimo pussy is very cold."[38]

Kubrick does not suggest that all refugees from extreme discipline and wars without fronts respond in the same way to such drills, arbitrary authority, exhaustion, and insults. Indeed, one slow learner, selected to be camp scapegoat by the drill sergeant, finally crosses to the dark side, shooting the sergeant and then himself; others do become killing machines; a few start wearing peace signs. "Joker," the narrator, takes to wearing both a sign on his helmet announcing himself to be a killing machine and a peace symbol on his vest. When asked why by a new commanding of-

38. For a recent update on practices and deaths at Parris Island, see https://www.washingtonpost.com/news/checkpoint/wp/2016/09/29/they -put-us-through-hell-a-marine-abused-at-boot-camp-explains-why-he -spoke-out/?utm_term=.f70537db3f61.

ficer, he replies, to "represent the duality of man, Sir!" What the soldiers share across those differences, however, is a heightened intensity of being that can make them angerous to themselves or others. The private militia, many urban police departments, numerous security officers, and some veterans groups carry such intensities into domestic life, ready to ignite an ugly movement if other conditions are right.

During and after the Trump election, there has been an upsurge of white racist groups prepared to adopt vigilante tactics on the slightest pretext. So far there is little sign that Jeffery Sessions or Donald Trump cares about monitoring them or enforcing established laws against them. These two instead seek to roll back recent Justice Department agreements with several city police forces to reverse the casual ways young black youths have been harassed and shot by a frighteningly large number of cops around the country.

Consider, in a slightly more systematic way, how right-wing publicists of the white evangelical movement in America speak to civilian "male warriors"—often enough veterans—who feel both squeezed out of the pluralistic life festering around them and deserving of compensatory entitlement for the lives they lead as high school–educated dudes in an economy that increasingly reserves decent job security and income for those with high-tech training. The idea is that the pressures, economic insecurities, tedious work schedules, military service, and repeated slights that mark their lives entitle them to special treatment by wives and children on the home front. That sense of compensatory entitlement, in turn, can foment white working-class rage against blacks, Muslims, Mexicans, gays, and feminists if and when such constituencies are blamed by demagogues for the injuries they suffer. The volatility of white rage.

It may be pertinent to note how some academics with upper-middle-class backgrounds skate over binds faced by portions of the white working class, even when the academics carefully explore the circumstances of other constituencies in even worse shape. Sometimes they may do so because it is assumed that the working class will eventually respond to its real class interests; sometimes because the bearers of working-class resentments must not be allowed to disrupt the precarious and variable pluralizing achievements of blacks, gays, transgender movements, women, and religious minorities; sometimes because it is thought that working-class men must now accept a diminished role in Democratic Party politics as the result of demographic changes. Different routes to different degrees of benign neglect. Other academics may slide in that direction because they are so pleased to have escaped a past that does not appeal to them. I understand that last temptation.

At one talk to a gender rights group a couple of years ago, when I posed a few issues of this sort, I was more or less told politely by some that white workers have to accept a new position in a new world. Well, yes, this class must be brought to terms with several vibrant pluralizing movements, but, no, not with the escalation of its job insecurities, its subjection to authoritarian bosses, its difficulties in getting and holding mortgages, or its declining ability to send its kids to good schools and colleges in an economy in which a high school education is not enough.

As such modes of benign neglect are wheeled into place—punctuated by justified outrage when extremists inside the neglected constellation take violent action—a set of aspirational fascists has been savvy at grasping the existential grievances gripping many in this constellation and attracting a faction of it toward neofascism. George Gilder, Rush Limbaugh, Bill O'Reilly, Sean Hannity, and Ann Coulter have served as leading cheerleaders across several decades of intense media agitation, with each adopting a rhetorical style bearing family resemblances to that more recently adopted by Donald Trump.[39] Several now admire Vladimir Putin as a "strong

39. One early study to powerfully capture this dynamism in midstream, discussing several of the names on my list, is Linda Kintz, *Jesus and the Market* (Durham, N.C.: Duke University Press, 1997). Another very

man," meaning one who rules through corruption, *kompromat*, imprisonment of his adversaries, and murder of his critics.

They have joined evangelicals to forge what I called in 2005 an "evangelical/capitalist resonance machine."[40] That machine encourages young white males to identify upward with males of economic power, supports white triumphalism and racism, often identifies America as a Christian nation, defines women to be subordinate, and has sought to draw the working-class contingent toward a neoliberal image of a market economy—all in the purported interest of returning to an early period of greatness. Here is the way I earlier enunciated one manifestation of this complex, concentrating on its evangelical instantiation. You may hear its echoes in recent speeches given by Donald Trump:

> The political formula of the Christian right is capped by defining men to be vulnerable, persecuted warriors in the capital-state system. They must receive special compensation for the ordeals they undergo, if the most creative, godly economy the world has ever seen is to flourish. Defining (putatively) natural differences between men as warriors and women as civilizers, George Gilder plays to resentments that many white working and middle class men feel as they are caught between the success of a traditional male elite and the more recent entry of professional women into its lower reaches. The message is that men must receive deference and special compensations if they are to sacrifice the warrior mentality natural to them to the higher civilizational imperatives of risky capitalist enterprise and stable family life. This is the fraught context, perhaps, in which new intensities of male support for guns, hunting, prisons, military campaigns, public expenditures for prisons, football stadiums, the military, and heterosexual normality are to be placed.[41]

---

recent study charts how the Nazi movement in its early stages drew explicitly upon anti-immigrant and eugenic policies in the United States from the late 1890s until the mid-1920s. See James Q. Whitman, *Hitler's American Model: The United States and the Making of Nazi Race Law* (Princeton, N.J.: Princeton University Press, 2017).

40. William E. Connolly, "The Evangelical-Capitalist Resonance Machine," *Political Theory,* December 2005, 869–88.

41. Quoted from Connolly, *Capitalism and Christianity, American Style,* 32.

It is not only that 82 percent of white evangelicals voted for Trump in 2016; most white police officers, prison guards, veterans, rural workers, private security workers, and soldiers did too. They also were enthusiasts at Trump rallies. During periods of uncertainty, they can be influential beyond their numbers in church assemblies, police union meetings, veterans groups, prison guard conversations, gun clubs, political rallies, neighborhood conversations, hunting parties, factory talk, nationalist groups, blog and Facebook posts, bar talk, and militia organizations. During each recent election, working-class factories in the Rust Belt have been flooded with late-breaking rumors about how the Democratic candidate would take away all hunting rifles.

As George Gilder asserted explicitly in another iteration of the political formula sketched earlier, the right-wing rhetoric he enunciates often taps lightly same-sex attractions among males, demands denial of such attractions, and finally draws upon the energies congealed to encourage working-class men to identify upward with ruthless corporate and military figures as visible models of prowess and power. Theweleit has already delineated how such strategies work.

The situation characterized in that 2005 essay has become more severe today. Many male warriors have now edged closer to aspirational fascism. More enraged men have become less patient with neoliberal trade agreements; more belligerent in their critiques of feminism, Muslims, blacks, Hispanics, academics, homosexuals, and the media; and more prepared to nudge the neoliberal side of the old machine consolidated in the early 1980s toward aspirational fascism.

Donald Trump, in his taped conversation about how he could get away with "grabbing pussy" because he is a celebrity, pulls several of these sentiments toward aspirational fascism. To him, a vagina is at once a target of predatory activity, a site of periodic bleeding that offends his demand for an antiseptic life, and a sign of a trophy to be paraded in front of male supporters as an unattainable object of desire. Spike heels become the order of the day. The parade of objects of unattainable desire, choreographed carefully, pulls aggrieved men toward Trump as it transfigures resentment against appealing elite women into identification with a man who asserts entitlement to them. Endless repetitions of such parades are critical, and the media happily complies with the expectation. This is Trump's crude revisitation of the choreography we encountered in that early modern ballet. Free Melania.

Many members of the white working class joined a host of other men and women in being profoundly offended by Trump's taped comments about women. They tapped into one side of that duality identified by "Joker" in *Full Metal Jacket*. Unfortunately, however, the Trump formula does speak to a subset of men. Our forays into a few affinities across differences between armored males in the early days of German fascism and white armored males sprinkled differentially across classes and regions in America today help us to understand why.

The difficult task is how to oppose aspirational fascism today as you draw a larger section of white working- and middle-class males into a pluralist, pluralizing, equalizing, and eco-economizing culture of democracy. Until a real dent is made in shaping a counteragenda, the dangerous, impulsive Trump may or may not be run out of office. But the constituencies and energies that call his ilk into being will continue to fester even if he is run out, ready to be tapped either to grab the reins of power or to persist as an implacable opposition to stifle the possibility of positive action by democratic means. Recall how armed white men suddenly appeared at public events just a few months after Barack Obama gained office, signaling to Republican officials entangled with them a belligerent demand to intensify rightwing obduracy in the face of the first African American president.

The task of recasting democracy, egalitarianism, and pluralism during a period when the aspiration to fascism is on the rise will be pursued in the next chapter. In the meantime, we close with one more set of quotations from Theweleit that might suggest resonances across differences between armored soldier males in pre-Nazi Germany, segments of white working-class males in America today, and the pugnacious, oh so antiseptic bearing of Donald Trump. To listen again to these comments is to recall how they denigrate both women and other minorities with whom fascist movements associate fluid and messy dimensions of life. Men trained bodily to feel this way are encouraged to call up traces of "feminine" feelings in themselves, as a precursor to hardening themselves again against such feelings. Indeed, the male lead in *Fifty Shades of Grey* displays that combination. And so does Donald Trump. Perhaps as we read the quotations that follow, we can recall how Trump, during the 2016 campaign, said that Megyn Kelly, the Fox newscaster, had been "bleeding from her eyes, her nose . . . , from everywhere" when she questioned the germophobe about the appalling things he had said about several women. The late June 2017 tweet asserting that Mika Brzezinski, a MSNBC journalist critical of Trump, was bleeding from her neck when recovering from plastic surgery adds another example to that list. Theweleit:

> When confronted with women, by contrast, their impulse is to pierce the facade of female "innocence" to display the whole morass of blood and excrement in which they perceive the female womb to be transformed in sexual intercourse, menstruation or childbirth. . . .
>
> In this sense the perception of the "bloody miasma" [from battle] becomes a form of revenge extracted from the mother as whore and child-bearer, or from the erotic sister-whore who betrays the brother. . . .
>
> Similarly, the "empty space" presents the soldier male with a permissible vision of the purified body of the devivified "white woman"—a vision stripped of the agitated mass of erotic female flesh, and its teeming inhabitants.[42]

42. Theweleit, *Male Fantasies*, 2:279. I should note that I have not reviewed how Theweleit argues against generic interpretations of fascist soldiers as repressed homosexuals. He finds Brecht and Adorno, on the Left, to be troublesome carriers of this disease. The idea is that once you acknowledge same-sex relations to be healthy aspects of a pluralist and pluralizing culture, you can see that some armored soldiers were active in same-sex relations, others were repressed, others yet were involved in heterosexual relations, and so forth. No single erotic object marks the fascist soldier male. Adorno today would surely reset the orientations to race and gender expressed in *Authoritarian Personality*.

Democracy, Plurality, and Class Inequality

Explanation and Evaluation

Is to explain also to justify or excuse? That charge comes up when people, with understandable impatience, yell that they have heard enough explanation about constituencies who impose so much grief on others. It is time for opposition, accusation, judgment, and conviction, given the injuries the offending parties have produced. This, indeed, is a risk that explanation runs when it addresses horrific, dangerous phenomena such as imperial conquest, criminality, murder, homophobia, racism, misogyny, classism, and fascism.

Actually, the risk points in at least two directions. The language of social explanation is unavoidably loaded with normatively coded terms of description. For instance, to describe something as a "mistake" rather than, say, either as intended directly or as an "accident" is to explain the behavior in ways that offer some limited mitigation for what happened. The agent intended to punish an infraction when in fact the punished party was innocent of the charge. When we see that language, as the dominant vehicle of social explanation and interpretation, is saturated by descriptive terms with normative edges—terms such as democracy, fascism, freedom, agency, responsibility, nation, and sovereignty—we can say that one risk of explanation is that it can be turned into a mass of accusations whereby the behavior in question is reduced to a list of indictments. That is, indeed, a risk fascists are all too happy to convert into a defining principle of political engagement with every group they despise, be they Jews, Poles, Muslims, Mexicans, blacks, homosexuals, the media, independent women, or the professoriate. Their favored words, such as scum, parasite, maggot, and degenerate, convey thin explanations linked to total indictments. It is nothing to squash a maggot seen as a threat to the aggressive, untrammeled identity you pursue. Hitler's explanation of the German loss in World War I as a "stab in the back" assumes this shape. It explains the loss as otherwise unnecessary—a stab—so as to blame labor and to prepare a future regime to bring labor to heel.

Unfortunately, some purveyors of identity politics today succumb to a variant of the first risk, though not to such an extreme degree. They are morally offended by this or that mode of behavior, as they often should be, but then fail to explore how to relieve the offense without only castigating, punishing, or excluding the offenders. Identity politics, you might say, confines the ethos of pluralism severely as it trumps too quickly the hard work of presumptive receptivity across differences and negotiation with a moralized politics of accusation. It is critical to identify fatal threats to pluralism that must be opposed. But a spray gun approach to accusation and condemnation insulates the accusers from seeking ways to transfigure antagonistic identity assertions into an ethos of relational pluralism and pluralization.

The temptation to simplicity in morality is a recipe for cruelty. It engenders constituency self-comfort at the expense of others whose injuries and grievances are not heard. It is not, however, that a pluralistic ethos of politics can or should be open to everything. It must sometimes, as we have noted before and will explore again, forge a pluralist assemblage of resistance to unitarian drives to the nation and, above all, to aggressive fascist drives to the internal and external racism of a ruthless, aggressive nation. These latter movements intend to decimate pluralism. Protests, town meetings, electoral campaigns, and, in severe situations, a general strike composed of several constituencies are needed here.[1]

---

1. In *Facing the Planetary,* chapter 5, I explore how a politics of swarming could morph into cross-regional support for general strikes composed of a plurality of constituencies to fend off the worst effects of

That returns us to the corollary risk of explanation. It is that explanation, by its terms of articulation, may excuse the offensive behavior explained. That, certainly, is a risk run in this study. The armored males we have engaged, some may say, are given too many excuses to be what they are through accounts of the disciplines injected into their lives.

One initial way to respond to the second risk is to join others in calling out blatant forms of misogyny, racism, endo-colonialism, militarism, fossil fuel infatuation, and aspirational fascism when you encounter them. Such responses to egregious offenses are both indispensable and insufficient, however. They are needed because standards of agency, responsibility, and accountability are essential to a pluralistic civilization. They are insufficient because reflective accounts can introduce proposals, say, to overcome the production of armored males at several sites in the future.

Those of us who pursue an ethic of cultivation—rather than either a morality of transcendent command or one of intrinsic obligation—must articulate norms of freedom, obligation, presumptive care, and responsibility that people who attain a threshold of adulthood can and should meet in pluralistic society. I have advanced such an articulation elsewhere.[2] The complexity that accompanies that project, however, is that agency, norms, and obligations are now acknowledged to be emergent formations that could not be unless the agents had been entangled in messy modes of child rearing, disciplines, wars, affective communications, feelings of distress, shocking or delirious events, and educational processes that enable them to be. The beatings, caresses, subliminal

---

accelerating climate change. It is easy to see how it can be adjusted to fit the struggle between pluralism and aspirational fascism.

2. See Connolly, *Fragility of Things,* chapter 3. That chapter contrasts the intercoded notions of moral agency, time, freedom, and responsibility in Kant with those offered by advocates of an ethic of cultivation in a world of becoming. Those latter orientations are those endorsed in this study, though as a pluralist, I also seek engagements with Kantians and neo-Kantians who draw from other moral sources.

influences, parental losses, days of hunger, family feuds, school
instruction, ego ideals, joys, griefs, and shocking events you are
exposed to in life enter somehow into the subject you become.
Perhaps you saw a father who came home from work every day
worn down by drudgery. Perhaps struggling parents left you to
be raised by grandparents in a challenging setting. Perhaps the
silo life you led within a gated community encouraged generosity
within its confined setting, punctuated by blind neglect of everything and everyone else. If the subject is a thing of this world, each
specific mode of achievement is shot through with some attitudes
and prejudgments in need of work to bring the operative ethos
of intersubjectivity and pluralism into closer accord. Such ambi-
guities in the ethos of the subject, on the reading advanced here,
form part of the human condition.

We can see retrospectively today, for instance, how the valuable
accounts of the authoritarian and manipulative personalities advanced by Adorno et al. in 1950 were themselves infected by tacit
attitudes about blacks, gays, and women in need of repair and reconstitution by those pursuing a culture of multifaceted democracy. That study appeared before the intense political activism of
the 1970s and 1980s pressed people and institutions to reconsti-
tute several extant understandings and norms. The subordinate
standing of women, for instance, is an expectation folded into that
text; breaks in it are treated as shining exceptions rather than new
norms in the making to be embraced. Adorno, if he were alive today, may well call some of these attitudes he adopted "prejudices."
They can be subject to potential reconstitution because he did not
fall into the deeper morass of either the authoritarian or the manipulative self.

But what about the latter "types"? A complex issue is in play
here. The very modes of induction by which an authoritarian personality acquires agency have been infiltrated by destructive af-
fects and tendencies often amplified by the groups in which they
move, while the beings they have become typically carry some
potential to work tactically upon themselves to rework those in-

stincts. That ambiguity warrants critics in calling the behavior out and working to inhibit its general expression. But that is not enough. Those who do so must also attend to institutional disciplines and bodily practices that help to draw such tendencies into being. A complex ethic of relational subjectivity requires its bearers to walk and chew gum at the same time. The issues are bodily, intersubjective, and institutional as well as subjective and ethical.

In such instances, to interpret is not to excuse. It can be to identify practices that help spawn the drives to aspirational fascism so that the fight against it can be better waged on more fronts: family life, schools, state policy, military training, corporations, police departments, churches, juridical penalties, localities, prisons, electoral politics, and social movements are candidates to be put into play here.

When such complexities are adumbrated, a few may be tempted to clear the decks with a simple model of intrinsic morality governed by a clean list of dictates and punishments. But that response encounters severe risks of its own, as we have begun to see. The authoritarian personality, for instance, views itself to be an agent of high morality in a world otherwise filled with immorality. That morality is simple, direct, and punitive: same-sex relations are wrong and perverts indulging in them must be punished; African Americans located low on the hierarchy of work and income deserve to be there; those who are not God fearing cannot be moral; and so on. In a moralistic morality, fixed judgment and accusation trump everything else.

One key lesson here is that immorality is not merely lodged in sin or self-interest. It can also be lodged in the very shape your moral conscience has assumed prior to close, caring, listening engagements with others who are on the receiving end of that conscience. Even the conscience-driven Immanuel Kant imported into his morality orientations to race, women, capital punishment, "filthy desert girls," and non-Western civilizations that would make any pluralist blush with shame today. Those conscience-driven dispositions were not mere cultural prejudices to be extricated from the moral universalism he pursued; they were sewn into the fabric of the universal philosophy by which he justified the purity of the "moral point of view," with its concomitant obligation to assume a linear, long history of "unbroken" civilizational progress.[3]

Sometimes it is insufficient to be ashamed of your immorality; sometimes it is important to become ashamed of some dictates of morality wired into your conscience. And that conscience often carries ties of loyalty to the constituencies to which you belong. Luckily, emergent feelings of care and shame, on one side, and the shape of official morality, on the other, are not always sewn that tightly together, so the inflow of new experiences can allow us to draw upon the former strains to rework aspects of the latter.

The logic of ethical life is inscribed with binds that are not always easy to negotiate. Pluralists I admire the most respond to this awareness by construing ethics to be a thing of this world, by working periodically to expose and counter unnecessary injuries embedded in the dominant constitution of conscience, by cultivating presumptive care for the protean diversity of being, by initiating political action to fold injuries heretofore outside the reach of conscience into conscience itself, by acknowledging the ethical subject to be an ambiguous achievement itself periodically in need of selective reconfiguration, by concurring that the presumption of generosity must sometimes be interrupted through formation of a militant pluralist assemblage to protect pluralism from a hostile fascist takeover, and by acknowledging, without deep resentment, that the basic sources of ethics from which they draw sustenance are themselves contestable in the eyes of many others.

When a pluralistic culture flourishes, you do not encounter merely diverse interests and identities; you also work to modify

3. See the dissertation by Adam Culver, "Race and Romantic Visions: A Tragic Reading" (PhD diss., Johns Hopkins University, April 2015), in which he shows how Kant's promulgation of a universal racial hierarchy is entrenched in some aspects of the moral philosophy he advances.

the secular demand that differences of fundamental faith must always be sequestered in the private realm so that reason can rule in the public realm. Deep pluralists doubt that such an antiseptic public reason suffices to do the job. Rather, Christians, Jews, Muslims, Hindus, Kantians, Amerindians, and nontheists of various sorts welcome a world, if they are pluralists, in which a multiplicity of ethical sources provides one of the operative conditions of being. William James would call this, perhaps, the first step toward deep pluralism. That, too, is a disposition that informs this study.[4] It stands as one way to counter fascist movements in which the accusatory mode and defilement of others trump every other disposition.[5]

Democracy and Pluralism

Jean-Jacques Rousseau treated wide diversity to be an enemy of democracy. A real democracy aims at a community of sentiments and obligations to which all, in the ideal case, can agree when they think about the benefit to the whole and not only their private interest. Only then can all citizens obey laws that they themselves have freely made. He eventually came to see that to approach such a condition, severe social disciplines would be

4. See William James, *A Pluralistic Universe* (Lincoln: University of Nebraska Press, 1996). A recent study by Alex Livingston carries the themes and ruminations of James into the resistance to imperialism. See Livingston, *Damn Great Empires: William James and the Politics of Pragmatism* (Oxford: Oxford University Press, 2016).

5. For a reflective defense of democracy against neoliberalism, see Wendy Brown, *Undoing the Demos* (New York: Zone Books, 2015). I admire this study in its attention to the Foucauldian modes of discipline that accompany neoliberalism and its exploration of neoliberal invasions of education. However, the image of democracy Brown advances, while egalitarian, may not be pluralistic on as many fronts as needed, particularly with respect to the intrinsic torsion between pluralism and pluralization and to the positive role of affective communication.

needed.[6] Communal democracy is an intense mode of disciplinary democracy.

Several ideals of democratic sovereignty are organized around different variants of such an existential demand, stated either as a realizable goal or as a regulative ideal to govern democratic politics even if it can never be realized completely. Several ideals of democratic collectivism take this form. Alternative studies expose a series of ugly disciplines and limits sewn into the fabric of such ideals, with the demand that the male sit in the seat of authority as head of the heterosexual family to give it unity often being first among them and a concentric image of culture in which the nuclear family, locality, and nation resonate back and forth, completing the picture.[7]

Franz Neumann and Hannah Arendt both teach, in different ways, how pluralism becomes an early casualty of fascism. Hitler worked assiduously to destroy independent labor unions, and he soon tracked most major social forums with a party-controlled organization to monitor and govern it. Police forces, courts, labor groups, universities, artistic organizations, state bureaucracies, schools, and youth forums faced parallel units aimed at rooting out "degeneracy" everywhere.[8] Even the family, officially beloved by the regime, lost much of its internal authority to schools and youth organizations designated to report deviations to the authorities. The fascist model pursues the utopia of an aggressive, concentric

6. For an impressive engagement with Rousseau on this issue, see Steven Johnston, *Encountering Tragedy: Rousseau and the Project of Democratic Order* (Ithaca, N.Y.: Cornell University Press, 1999).

7. For a thoughtful study that probes this territory, and allied territory as well, see Bonnie Honig, *Democracy and the Foreigner* (Princeton, N.J.: Princeton University Press, 2001).

8. William Sheridan Allen, in *The Nazi Seizure of Power* (New York: Franklin Watts, 1984), provides a detailed examination of how several "parallel" Nazi units consolidated rule over one German town, Northeim, during the early phase of Nazi takeover. He also reviews how the social democrats put up a good fight until they were dispersed through rumor, terror, arrests, and rejection by neighbors.

ideal of a racial nation with enthusiastic masses at the bottom, punitive party organizations in the middle, and an unquestionable Führer at the top. The transfiguration of more benign, concentric images of culture—replete with their own serious exclusions—into an aggressive, fascistic order.

Neumann and Arendt, however, both had somewhat different images of pluralism than that projected here. Neumann identified a pluralism of group interests, with labor and capital dominant among them. He thought that this model of pluralism was rickety and unsustainable as long as deep, structural conflicts between labor and capital built into the capitalist system as such remained intact. Did he aspire to replace pluralism with a benign model of collectivism?

Arendt invokes "natality" to appreciate how we enter a world filled with a plurality of perspectives to be negotiated somehow. This plurality exceeds a plurality of "interests," eventually projecting a diversity of metaphysical assumptions, existential hopes, and political demands. Fascism, she showed, supplanted such an evanescent plurality with its own variant of "a classless society." This was not a classless society of communism with its radical reduction of economic inequality and projection of communal harmony through the demise of private profit. Fascism was designed to squash that model of classlessness while siphoning the political energies it had fomented into an alternative ideal. Fascist classlessness retained a sharp hierarchy between capital, the middle class, and labor while inspiring Aryans to reach beyond such trivial divisions to the higher unity of a racial *Volk*. That unity, in turn, was to be pursued through relentless attacks on external regimes and degenerates inside that obstructed racial unity: non-Aryan "peoples," Jews, homosexuals, Romani, Poles, social democrats, and communists very high on that list. The latter two were targeted in large part because they were both highly organized and pursued ideals of classlessness that resisted the racial *Volk* ideal.

Arendt herself eventually moved toward a more contained image of pluralism in which face-to-face meetings allow people in limited settings to "enact" something new. She searched for rare settings in which plurality and creativity could meet in politics.[9] A noble quest—perhaps designed to protect a vision of pluralism during difficult times—though it did not grapple closely with the issue within and across large-scale societies.

Neither Neumann nor Arendt imagined another important dimension of pluralism—in fact, Arendt resisted it—that is, acknowledgment of a plurality of agencies of different sorts within and beyond the human estate through which much of the earth is composed. During the current age of the Anthropocene, this last dimension of pluralism must be engaged widely and deeply. So I very much respect how Neumann and Arendt exposed the fascist attack on pluralism. But I pursue a wideband pluralism that probably neither would embrace in all its dimensions.[10]

A key lesson to be remembered from both, however, is that fascism is anathema to pluralism in any of its forms and that any democracy worth its salt must strengthen itself by folding multifaceted diversities into it. Good night, Jean-Jacques Rousseau. Good morning, William James and Judith Butler.[11]

9. See Hannah Arendt, *Between Past and Future* (Oxford: Penguin, 2006). For a study that is both indebted to Arendt and revises her thinking in a way suited to the large scale of contemporary life, see Bonnie Honig, *Public Things: Democracy in Disrepair* (New York: Fordham University Press, 2017).

10. For an essay that shows how Neumann became more of a pluralist in his later work, see Christian Fuchs, "The Relevance of Franz Neumann's Critical Theory in 2017," *Triple C* 15, no. 2 (2017): 637–50, http://www.triple -c.at/index.php/tripleC/article/viewFile/903/1025.

11. You might find James, *A Pluralistic Universe,* and Butler, in *Precarious Life,* to inform and complement one another. James advances a philosophy of time as becoming amid multiple modes of agency, including humans and nonhumans, to inform multifaceted pluralism; Butler appreciates the role that vulnerability plays in ethical life and in igniting social movements to support wider bands of plurality in human affairs. I feel indebted to both.

The Powers of Multifaceted Pluralism

We will explore soon the indispensable element of egalitarianism. For now, let's elaborate a multifaceted image of democratic pluralism that is noble in itself and, once tethered to egalitarianism, better equipped than other modes to fend off recurrent temptations to both concentric nationalism and, its extreme cousin, fascism. Either of those temptations can coalesce into a movement after this or that jolt disrupts a regime. You can even say that democratic pluralism contains frustrations amid its wonders that periodically foment fantasies of unity and fullness. These are the limits to which a pluralist order must become adjusted. Pluralism challenges several quests for simplicity, fullness, unity, purity, and community, while also resisting calls to market society and radical individualism.

Let us set periodic elections, court and popular commitment to equal voting rights, a strong legislature, and periodic practices of citizen activism and agitation as at once critical to democracy and essential to consolidation of its pluralist mode. Several dimensions of multifaceted pluralism express such conditions and consolidate them further.

First, a wide range of faiths, identities, interests, and aspirations form key ingredients in a regime of democratic pluralism. We speak of the ideal now and not of obvious ways existing regimes fall below it. A positive ethos of engagement between constituencies, with each including members with ties to several others, conveys a delicate balance between asserting the rights and demands of each and listening to grievances and initiatives of others that had heretofore been shelved. Such modes of listening become folded into the public ethos, partly because each constituency needs others to push its own agenda, partly because many allow presumptive care for others to be folded into their priorities, and partly because new movements periodically publicize grievances and goals previously overlooked by many. Gays need health care for spouses at their place of work; African Americans in the city often need better schools and work opportunities; many in the working class need, say, better job security, health care, and working conditions; women need access to professions previously closed to them; small entrepreneurs need state subsidies to initiate eco-friendly ventures; high school graduates need access to dignified modes of work that allow them to raise families, buy a house, and send their kids to a decent school; nontheists need opportunities to express their faiths in the public square; and so on indefinitely. These diverse claims do not reflect an equality of need, but in a pluralist order, each can be put into play.

So pluralism is a practice replete with uncertain balances and connections among diverse constituencies. A general ethos that incorporates appreciation of the fragility of things is, indeed, one element conducive to a pluralist order. And, as we shall soon see, that appreciation needs to stretch out to nonhuman beings and planetary forces as well as extending beyond the internal dynamics of pluralist politics in a territorial state.

Second, the broad bandwidth of a pluralist ethos is critical. Such an ethos, set both on the affective register of communication and more reflective processes, injects powers of critical responsiveness and resilience into politics. A positive ethos of pluralist engagement—in which the virtues of initiating and listening oscillate back and forth between constituencies—must find expression in diverse bodily practices that encourage a constituency to dilate at some moments and tighten at others. Those invested with pluralistic sensibilities may work upon their gaits, habits of eye contact, exposure to unfamiliar experiences, periodic modes of meditation, and practices of devotion, doing so to pour an affirmative ethos of engagement into the timbre of bodily relations and refinements of soul. For, as the history of fascism teaches, there is never a vacuum on the cultural register of bodily demeanor and affective communication.

A broadband ethos of presumptive generosity within and across constituencies is noble in itself; it also provides one of the fundamental forces to ward off hostile fascist takeovers when they arise.

Recent work on mirror neurons and the proliferation of olfactory sensors in different parts of the human organism suggest how practices of dilation do their work at the visceral level of being. You prime, say, your dream life before going to sleep, and the dreams that unfold both ignite different olfactory sensors and prepare the self to respond in new ways to an issue the next day.[12] You expose yourself to unfamiliar constituencies on both the registers of sensory and intellectual life. Work upon relational bodily processes paves the way to deepen an ethos of pluralist engagements; it can also, if pursued in a very different style, foster armored bodies intent on cutting off multifaceted pluralism at the pass. Police departments, military organizations, private militia, gun clubs, football teams, college fraternities, and football fans can be susceptible—to varying degrees—to the latter practices.

Of course, bodily work is insufficient, as can be seen when practices of generosity within a confined constituency encounter shocks when others outside the charmed circle express a grievance. The silo lives of the very rich and the narrow school and neighborhood associations in some white working- and middle-class zones can easily foster an ethos of confined generosity.

A pluralist ethos of positive engagement is not, though, limited to the visceral register of cultural life. That would not make its bandwidth broad enough. It must also find ample expression in conceptually refined journalistic, academic, church, regional, gender, race, class, and ethnic articulations. It includes an ideological element. We call upon each other to listen at one moment, to initiate at another, and to agitate at yet another. When there is a decent fit between the array of bodily practices and conceptually refined articulations, the bandwidth of a pluralist ethos grows.

12. One suggestive article here is Sandeep Ravindran, "Senses in Unlikely Places," *The Scientist,* Summer 2016, 51–58. Jane Bennett is now preparing a study of subliminal "in-fluences" of multiple sorts that enter bodily demeanor below the senses and conscious attention that draws on such examples.

The consolidation of a broadband ethos does not mean, of course, that people easily come to agreement on defining issues of the day. No political regime in fact provides that guarantee, though some pretend to do so. The sought result often requires a combination of negotiation, goodwill, and creativity on the part of diverse constituents exposed to different degrees of suffering and privilege. The strange demand to find a guarantee in advance for sovereignty, public agreement, or rational decision engenders the temptation to heap contempt upon pluralism, democracy, equality, and "parliamentarism." Hitler, as we have seen, held all four in contempt. Stalin did too. So do Steve Bannon and Stephen Miller.

Politics, by its mode of being, comes replete with real uncertainties. In a pluralist regime, each constituency, as a regulative ideal, listens to others at some moments and periodically pursues initiatives that jostle them at others. Pluralism solicits an ethos of agonistic respect across intersecting constituencies in which several pursue the possibility of reaching peaceable settlements. Pluralism is thus an adversary of purity, whether the latter assumes the voice of moral purity, the concentric nation, radical individualism, or aspirational fascism. We, remember, speak of an ideal now, not the actual systems that break with it in various ways.

The third feature of democratic pluralism stands in a relation of interdependence and tension with the first. That should not be too surprising, because multifaceted pluralism consists of relations of interdependence and tension between facets of several sorts. That also helps to constitute its resilience. The third feature consists of periodic struggles for pluralization or becoming that disturb the intersections between already established constituencies as it places new pressure on established system priorities.

In an established pluralist order, a loosely defined set of rights will be recognized, a variety of faiths can anticipate respect, multiple identities can participate in the public square, and several constituencies will have interests to protect. But, periodically, a demand bubbles up to add a new right, faith, identity, or end to the mix previously subjected to obscurity or abjection. Some of these initiatives may require minor adjustments, others a significant shift in the tone of institutional ethos and bodily practices, and others yet radical changes in the current system of jobs, authority, education, respect, and freedom reaching deeply into the organization of economic and spiritual life. These are periods of danger and possibility to pluralism.

Some pluralists contend that if a new claim to a right, faith, identity, or public end is to become legitimate, it must have already been implicit in the register of rights and faiths honored in a constitution or society that respects persons. Others, like me, contend that some new rights and identities are neither implicit nor discovered. They, rather, cross the threshold of legitimacy through a politics of struggle and real creativity. They rise—through a messy mix of intense political pressure and appeals to subterranean strains of care in others—from a place below the register of public legitimacy to a new place on the roster of respected rights and identities.

To say they were already "implicit," we think, depreciates the risky political struggles by which new rights and identities are created; it undermines appreciation of the role real creativity plays in politics; it encourages many to place themselves at the front end of a linear process of civilizational history by which the implicit has gradually become explicit; and it may engrain the will to obedience too deeply into cultural life, as obedience to the implicit assumes too much priority over other political virtues of creativity and struggle.

The notions of progress attached to a unilateral notion of the implicit are too linear and confined. Many of us were surprised in the past as a new claim was met and are apt to be surprised again. For new circumstances, events, problems, and suffering periodically generate new squeezes out of which urgent drives for the creation of new rights, identities, faiths, or ends emerge, that is, out of which a fork in cultural time unfolds. This is where the elements of uncertainty, struggle, care, and creativity meet in the dissonances of politics. And all four meet the possibility of new cultural achievements or tragedy.

Without an element of uncertainty, real creativity could not occur. Without an element of real creativity, politics is squeezed out of life. With both, however, tragic possibility also tracks politics. Additionally, when the political element is alive and well, consummate modes of explanation bump into their limits. Politics exceeds the powers of explanation while drawing upon those powers to explore platforms from which new experiments can be forged.

Consider some recent claims to add new rights or ends in a few democratic states: the right to doctor-assisted suicide, the right to practice nontheistic reverence in the public square, the right to same-sex marriage, the right to reparations for regions that have contributed the least and suffered the most from climate change— each is a right that has either been wrested from the body politic as people listened to a new claim or is now poised on the precarious edge of possibility.

To appreciate the politics of pluralization in this way may also encourage some pluralists to pour a sense of proliferating possibilities into the very ontology of being embraced. Or so say some of us, who are so obdurate in our commitment to pluralism that we pour it into a pluralist onto-cosmology. We think that the periodic experience of real creativity is critical to freedom and that, even with its risks, strains of creativity in life help to make it worth living.

But does this distinction between the implicit and the creative leave a mixed mode out? Perhaps some of these drives were creative, while others have been poised in an obscure zone of indiscernibility between the implicit and the created. For instance, one strain in the present might be extrapolated out until it encounters another heterogeneous strain that coalesces creatively with it. That, indeed, may be how life itself emerged out of a "coupling" of two trajectories with different potentialities. The demand for, say, doctor-assisted suicide in a high-tech medical order may have emerged out of a series of complex confluences between caring for dying parents and acquaintances, growing awareness of the ambiguous effects of new medical technologies on life, and emergent understandings that the old binary distinction between suicide and death by natural causes obscures a festering zone between those two blunt categories. A new situation, creativity, and new strains of care bubbling up together. Or, say, discovery of how carbon capitalism generates rapid climate change may help to engender new modes of planetary care and creative intervention in which carbon-producing states provide reparation funds to regions now suffering the most from the effects of the Anthropocene.

Debates between partisans of the implicit, the creative, and zones of indiscernibility between them are apt to continue in a pluralist society. Some parties to it may demand that the world itself consist of sharp demarcations so that their demand for rigor and definitive categories is redeemed by it. But that begs the question of whether it does. Other pluralists respect an element of messiness projected into the world itself. The debate between such perspectives, if pursued in the right spirit, contributes to multifaceted pluralism. When a pluralist order thrives, such debates form part of its ethos, even though their cutting edges do shift over time. Parties to them find it wise to form practical coalitions across those divergences from time to time. They practice a politics of agonistic respect in which people periodically debate deep things about time, divinity, interspecies perspectivism, and the degree to which the world itself is legible to our categorical formations, doing so without immediately demanding that every such debate be resolved in a definitive way.

One key to the politics of pluralization—in which a new claim becomes poised at a key moment on a tipping point at which it could cross the threshold to acceptance or recede into a place of obscurity or anger—is the bandwidth of a democratic, pluralist culture. When the bandwidth is broad, people initially disturbed by a new claim may stretch themselves to listen with new ears, bodily dilations and care. They may become open to inflows of unfamiliar experience. Perhaps a group of panicked men decides to work on bodily assumptions culturally wired into their sexual practices, until they reach a time, say, when transgender practices no longer threaten their capacity to "get it up." The politics of pluralization often reaches deeply into relational bodily practices. That helps to explain the intensity the politics of pluralization can generate for several on multiple sides of an issue.

The politics of pluralization explains further why advocates of an ethos of pluralism emphasize its connection to the bodily ethos of being. We know today, for instance, that many whites who transcend racism on the refined registers of reflection feel tremors of it in visceral zones when, say, encountering young blacks on a city street. One step on the rocky road to overcoming white triumphalism in the hierarchy of a capitalist society is to work on the visceral register of cultural life.

One attraction to fascism can arise when people first deny the importance of visceral processes to life and then fall into a panic when they encounter an unexpected claim. That is because the visceral register is often occupied by a set of tacit entitlements among those who look down upon constituencies below them on the social hierarchy. This is one lesson Rousseau taught well, when he grounded the stability of a stratified society in the ability of those bearing burdens imposed from above to find at least one other stratum below them to impose burdens upon in return. Except those on the bottom rung.

There are many things to do if and when you find yourself on the edge with respect to a live issue that bites into a set of consolidated bodily tendencies: go to films that display different habits of romance or race relations than those tacitly wired into your demeanor; join symposia, marches, and protests to support practices you have begun to think are legitimate but do not yet feel so very confidently; alter a few roles you practice in work, church, school, family, or local life to see what differences they make both to the world and to the solidity of your new disposition. Or, on another front, immerse yourself in the history of fossil fuel mining; review the horrendous effects those practices have had on regions outside old capitalist states and decimated zones within them; inhale the repulsive smells and devastated vista of an open air coal mining field as you study the effects fossil fuel regimes have on the galloping pace of planetary climate change. You address the issue on different, interfolded registers of being until perhaps a new feeling starts to bubble up. You may soon find that you have become a supporter of regional climate reparations and mitigations, now prepared to become more adventurous with others in collective movements on their behalf.

But must every demand for becoming cross such a magical threshold onto legitimacy? No, some must be rejected. We have reached the point, however, at which some defenders of morality as a set of intrinsic principles reach for their guns. They pretend that they can show their favored source of ethics to be more demonstrable than they can. Moreover, it is often possible to reach across creedal differences about the ultimate source of moral judgment and still decide together that child pornography is a destructive and unacceptable practice. Some may reach that conclusion because they find it to follow from intrinsic principles they endorse. Others may do so after consulting the vulnerabilities of young children, the care they themselves feel for the vulnerable, and the dark practices of trafficking that have become so active.

An ethic of cultivation linked to presumptive care for the diversity of being does not always come down immediately on the best answer. Neither, by the way, does a morality of divine command or one of Kantian necessity in a world in which contending authorities regularly assert themselves to be the final interpreter of its true dictates.

So some obdurate pluralists think it is important to balance those who think an intrinsic morality is the only route to follow. We do so because we are attuned to an ugly history of moral certainty: what was heretofore taken to be certain often becomes felt later to be a set of prejudices with unnecessary injurious effects on others installed in bodily practices and cultural regimes that could be altered. The claim that slavery reflects an unbreakable hierarchy of being, that only property owners are qualified to vote, that women must be confined to the household, that same-sex marriage is an assault on biology, that Western civilization represents the highest peak of human achievement, that you cannot be ethical unless you accept a progressive image of time—all these have been supported by appeals to an intrinsic code during some periods. So, some of us balance the potential dogmatism of intrinsic morality with an ethic of cultivation designed to contest it. Debates over ethical sources are apt to be interminable in a culture of broadband pluralism. Welcome to the planet earth.

The politics of pluralization tests the boundaries and resilience of broadband pluralism. It could not be otherwise, because the tensions between existing balances and a new aspiration are often severe. You may be pressed to modify some rights, assumptions, and bodily practices to which you are accustomed if this new right, identity, end, or faith is to be given room in the public square. Affirmative action in corporate boardrooms, universities, workplaces, local businesses, temples, cities, media presentations, and so on, may be essential to seed the way for more radical changes yet. As will become increasingly clear, I think the latter activities have the best chance of gaining momentum when a series of significant changes is made in the position of the working class as a whole.

A thick ethos of pluralization dramatizes elements of unacknowledged suffering, uncertainty, and fragility in politics. The key point to remember, however, is that other types of political regimes face such uncertainties without containing within themselves an ethos well equipped to address them. Classical theories of sovereignty are often plagued by this dilemma, partly because they strive to resolve it in advance rather than taking the pluralist route.[13]

This institutionalized tension between pluralism and pluralization constitutes a key way to fend off pressures to transfigure the rule of law into the law of rule that arises periodically in con-

13. I examine this issue within and across states in "The Complexity of Sovereignty," in *Sovereign Lives: Power in Global Politics,* ed. Jenny Edkins and Veronique Pin-Fat, 23–41 (London: Routledge, 2004).

centric cultures. When you recall how Hitler took advantage of strong cultural traditions toward obedience to the law—doing so to transfigure them into the law of rule—it becomes clear how this periodic tension between pluralism and pluralization constitutes a strength of multifaceted democracy. A presumptive acceptance of authority among diverse constituencies, periodically qualified in these ways, is less apt to become transfigured into a mass will to obedience.

The multifaceted image of pluralism so far advanced could be said to sit rather comfortably with this or that creed of human exceptionalism. Several late-modern pluralists, such as Arendt, Berlin, Shklar, Rawls, Dahl, Keynes, and Habermas, have been diverse carriers of such a tradition. An exceptionalist insists either that species evolution has created a rupture separating humanity radically from all other beings or that a God has endowed humanity with the right to govern the rest of nature. But many perspectivalists, both inside and outside northern capitalist states, have argued that the capacities of feeling, agency, reflection, and judgment in which Euro-Americans typically take so much pride are also distributed among other species. The debates between critics of exceptionalism and its defenders are numerous and cover many issues. For now it may suffice to say that broad perspectivalism appreciates a wide distribution of capacities and feelings extending well beyond human beings that many in northern states had heretofore treated as confined to humanity itself. Typically, such a sense of human uniqueness was then joined to a stark sense that northern, capitalist, democratic regimes express the highest version of these capacities among all civilizations, so that Mill, Locke, Tocqueville, Kant, Hegel, Marx, and Heidegger could—in their various ways—set "us" up to be a unique species and the North to sit at the pinnacle of that uniqueness so far attained in history.[14]

14. You can call such doctrines carriers of "sociocentrism" and "humanist exceptionalism." They have found expression in major currents of the humanities and human sciences in Euro-American life. These trends

What happens if and as more cultural pluralists acknowledge that either the Creator or the fecundity of immanence (or both) has endowed a host of animals, plants, and perhaps some other forces with differential powers of agency, feeling, communication, and judgment? Could such a differential be placed on a single scale or even expressed through a linear history of progress? Or does an onto-cosmology of proliferation make more sense here? Is it possible now to place an eccentric tradition in Euro-American thought (led perhaps by Sophocles, Lucretius, Nietzsche, James, Kafka, Whitehead, Deleuze, Grosz, Haraway, and Bennett) into closer communication with longer traditions of broadband perspectivalism in other parts of the world?[15] Several studies now pursue these issues with care and urgency. What happens to received notions of civilization, food supply, eating habits, clothing, tourism, agriculture, and faith when such an issue is explored deeply? Does my attitude to the crocodile, the whale, or the octopus shift significantly after I finally acknowledge that the first exercises complex modes of group communication below the decibel level of unaided human reception, the second communicates across thousands of miles in highly sophisticated ways, and the third exercises complex brain functions that scramble exceptionalist assumptions about how thinking and action must be organized to be thinking and action? What happens once I consult sensitive studies of interplant communication?

Such issues are proliferating today. No doubt, they disturb many who wish to save exceptionalism from challenge. But a widening

---

are, however, counterbalanced by a "minor" tradition in Euro-American life contesting such assumptions. There has been a surge of exchanges across the minor tradition in old capitalist states and versions of perspectivalism in southern regions. For one comparison between Amazonian perspectivalism, Gilles Deleuze, and Claude Lévi-Strauss, see Eduardo Viveiros de Castro, *Cannibal Metaphysics* (New York: Univocal, 2014).

15. Besides the classics noted, see Elizabeth Grosz, *Chaos, Territory, Art* (New York: Columbia University Press, 2008), and Jane Bennett, *Vibrant Matter* (Durham, N.C.: Duke University Press, 2010).

range of experience and study keeps flowing in, and it seems unwise to crawl into a cocoon to avoid the inflow. For now, it may suffice to say that advocates of multifaceted pluralism explore modes and types of nonhuman agency that exceptionalists had cast into the dustbin of history. Cultural pluralism now becomes invested with the entanglements of interspecies pluralism. We seek to become alert to a wider range of interdependencies and fragilities than exceptionalists had allowed us to encounter. Interspecies pluralism pursued during a period when the "sixth extinction" is well under way.

That brings us to the fifth dimension of multifaceted pluralism. Devotees of multifaceted pluralism are alert to the fragilities within which the practices they honor are set. We know that we periodically have to band together across differences of creed (e.g.., Christian, Hindu, Muslim, Kantian, Deleuzian, nontheistic, indigenous, and proceduralist), social position (class, age, ethnicity, etc.), and world region, doing so to forge affinities of spirituality that reach across distinctions of creed and social position, as we protect democratic cultures of pluralism from reductions and hostile takeovers. We know that the quest for fundamentalism, the intensely centered nation, white triumphalism, or fascism can escalate during periods of duress. It is just that we do not believe that centered nationalism or an authoritarian party provides the best way to respond to such challenges. For the latter risk emulating the condition they seek to oppose. As I argued in an earlier essay on "Fundamentalism in America," some of the same conditions that foster pluralist possibility open up temptations to antipluralist response.[16]

Some people in the past may have missed this element in my theory, though it has been a feature of it for decades. Why? Perhaps because some who focus upon the urgent need to resist

16. For earlier discussions of those drives and the urgent need for pluralist assemblages to resist them, see *Ethos of Pluralization,* chapters 3, 4, and 6, and *Capitalism and Christianity,* chapters 2 and 5. Two reasons to

hierarchical nationalism quickly conclude that such responses can only emerge from a highly unified party, class, constituency, or leader. But those movements produce the silo effect that is dangerous. So pluralists doubt that a single party, class, leader, or highly centered movement will turn the trick. To critical pluralists the best way to start is to pursue positive affinities of spirituality between constituencies drawn from multiple creeds and social positions.

Depending on the threat, such a multifaceted movement will assume a specific shape. If it is to support same-sex marriage, it may ignite several creedal constituencies to act upon themselves, their workplaces, the courts, their localities, and electoral politics—a politics of swarming in which success on a few fronts may trigger a tipping point. If race relations is the issue, the response may be to press on several fronts to redress severe obstacles African Americans face in the domains of criminal law, police enforcement, work, education, voting, the professions, higher education, and corporate life, while simultaneously relieving some of the conditions that encourage strains of racism in the white working class. It is to work on class and race hierarchies together. If the call is to act upon climate change—a grave danger that some regions have produced the most while others face the most immediate and severe effects—the critical assemblage must be composed of participants from several regions. The task is to pursue affinities of spirituality across differences of creed and social position. Perhaps such an assemblage could inspire a series of cross-regional general strikes to put intense pressure on offending states, corporations, universities, localities, and churches

---

attend to the condition of the white working and lower middle classes are that these improvements are important in themselves and preconditions to real improvements in the zones of race relations, sexual practices, and responses to the dangers of the Anthropocene. For a collection attending to several of these issues, see Davide Campbell and Morton Schoolman, eds., *The New Pluralism: William Connolly and the Contemporary Global Condition* (Durham, N.C.: Duke University Press, 2008).

from inside and outside at the same time. Certainly, during the era of Trump, radical action is needed.

In each case, multiple nodes of coordination will be assembled (unions, churches, states, international social movements, localities, regions, parties, etc.), but no central coordinator will be in command. Indeed, intense jostling for the position of command can destroy such movements. Effective assemblage movements, in fact, may be closer to how human body–brain processes actually work than to the treelike models of brain activity many neuroscientists are now leaving in the dust.

If the most salient threat becomes fascism, once again, the need is to work on several sites across multiple constituencies. A militant pluralist assemblage is the best way to counter the threat of fascism, doing so in ways that involve risk and courage as you avoid replicating the model of political organization the opposition pursues so relentlessly. You must, in this case too, work on bodily processes of communication as well as refined modes of articulation. For as we have seen, bodily drills form one of the keys to a fascist movement, joined to the Big Lies, rumormongering, authoritarianism, and terror that inform it.

Certainly several threats and dangers can feed into one another. A rapid change in the Antarctic ice cap, for instance, could intensify drives to fascism in several old capitalist states, generating urgent demands to build walls to resist refugee flows; fostering ugly military temptations; and intensifying race, gender, and class conflicts. The most dangerous source of fascist temptation today, perhaps, arises from the way rapid climate change generates drought, ocean acidification, denialism, food shortages, water emergencies, refugee crises, territorial rigidities, and war risks. Here too, a cross-regional pluralist assemblage provides the most promising mode of response.

So, five facets of democratic pluralism: multiple constituencies of several types, a broadband ethos of positive engagement installed in relational bodily dispositions and reflective articulations, a periodic politics of pluralization situated in a relation of torsion with the representational politics of pluralism, entangled ties with a plurality of agencies and volatile planetary forces that exceed the human estate, and periodic formation of militant pluralist assemblages to protect these rhizomatic complexes from hostile fascist takeovers—each facet reenforces the others as it also periodically subsists in tension with them.

Pluralist intersections (number 6) are also accompanied by a modicum of litter, noise, precarity, public things, nonhuman agencies, and forces that sometimes career out of place. Such is the condition of pluralism, as contemporary pluralist thinkers as diverse as Nidesh Lawtoo, Judith Butler, Bonnie Honig, Deborah Danowski, Eduardo Viveiros de Castro, Jane Bennett, Cornel West, Thomas Dumm, Jeffrey Isaac, Catherine Keller, Donna Haraway, Kathy Ferguson, and Édouard Glissant see and feel in overlapping ways.[17]

Clearly other elements could be added to this list of intersecting axioms. Indeed, we turn now to one—number 7—that must be in play if broadband democratic pluralism is to flourish.

17. I note important works that play positive roles in the perspective pursued here: Nidesh Lawtoo, *The Phantom of the Ego* (Lansing: Michigan State University Press, 2013); Deborah Danowski and Eduardo Viveiros de Castro, *The Ends of the World* (Oxford: Polity Press, 2016); Thomas Dumm, "The Problem of 'We'; or the Persistence of Sovereignty," *boundary 2*, Fall 1999, 55–64; Cornel West, *Race Matters* (New York: Vintage, 1994); Édouard Glissant, *Poetics of Relation*, trans. Betsy Wing (Ann Arbor: University of Michigan Press, 1928); Catherine Keller, *Cloud of the Impossible* (New York: Columbia University Press, 2014); Donna Haraway, *Staying with the Trouble: Making Kin in the Chthulucene* (Durham, N.C.: Duke University Press, 2016); Kathy Ferguson, *Emma Goldman's Political Thinking in the Streets* (New York: Rowman and Littlefield, 2013); Cornel West, *Democracy Matters: Winning the Fight against Imperialism* (New York: Penguin Books, 2005); and Jeffrey Isaac in recent posts in Public Seminar, http://www.publicseminar.org/, which have responded to Trump and threats to democracy. These authors and texts point to modes of pluralist proliferation at interrelated sites.

Capitalism, Pluralism, and Equality

Old capitalist states, as we have seen, periodically face the sting of nationalist, fascist, and neofascist movements, particularly after a crisis when an old set of entitlements is squashed or placed under intense pressure. Constituencies tempted in such directions can vary from time to time and place to place. My focus will be on constituency temptations, dangers, and possible responses to them in the United States, partly because I feel better qualified to delve into the issue here and partly because the United States is going through a dangerous period for itself and other regions of the world.

But why focus on the question of equality rather than other possibilities? Would not some others be easier to pursue? Well, this is the alternative that holds the best chance of drawing disaffected workers, families, homeowners, and consumers more actively into a pluralist assemblage. The other possibilities are apt to perpetuate the uneasy situation in which neoliberal and pluralist each attains hegemony in some domains, as they jointly create conditions ripe for the emergence of fascist rebellions. Pluralism, democracy, and egalitarianism need one another if all are to attain the needed resilience.

The considerations advanced here are informed by another assumption too: no capitalist order is ever sufficient to itself. Its multiple transactions with periodically volatile planetary forces, such as the ocean conveyor, glacier flows, drought incursions, species changes and extinctions, and climate change; its troubled relations with historically exploited regions; its entanglements with distinctive spiritualities inhabiting the intersecting institutions of family, temple, education, investment, work, profit, consumption, growth, and regulation—all these ensure the insufficiency of capitalism to itself.[18] So is the corollary fact that capitalism, too, fac-

18. In *The Idea of Socialism,* trans. Joseph Ganahl (Oxford: Polity, 2017), Alex Honneth pursues an ideal of socialism that expands the focus

es periodic encounters with surprising events that must be addressed: events such as a new war, a resource crisis, the collapse of an ally, a new social movement, a sudden speedup of a glacier melt, an emerging climate crisis, the discovery of a new energy source, a persisting drought, a subprime mortgage collapse, or a revolt in a previously subordinate region. Any structural theory of capitalism that downplays such diverse elements to gain the appearance of self-sufficiency is hardly worth the seminar discussions it generates.

Another way to put this is to say that capitalism finds variable modes of expression, so that Keynesian capitalism, neoliberal capitalism, the capitalism of an evangelical/neoliberal machine, Chinese one-party capitalism, and fascist capitalism represent merely five versions that are irreducible to one another. Yes, powerful forces in each seek to capture work, the state, art, erotic life, consumption, crime, religion, and investment priorities to serve the goals of capital, but the variations and degrees of difference between them are also significant. (Note that I did not say the interests of capital, because the recurrent history of capitalist meltdowns teaches us that capitalists often do not know their own interests.)

The generic drive of capital is to capture numerous activities for profit and control. But different types of capitalism allow different degrees, modes, and sites of capture.[19] A multifaceted culture of pluralism and pluralization provides resources to counter

---

on economic organization that weakened earlier theories. The engagements with Proudhon and Marx are very insightful. Families, feminist rights, and other issues are drawn into the mix. If he also were to emphasize, first, the essential torsion between established plurality and new drives to pluralization, second, the role that affective communication plays in a pluralist ethos of engagement, and, third, the urgent need today to overcome sociocentric assumptions in the human sciences, our two perspectives would move closer.

19. Note, e.g., the study by Lester Spence, *Knocking the Hustle: Against the Neoliberal Turn in Black Politics* (Brooklyn, N.Y.: Punctum Books, 2016). He charts how several black churches now adopt a neoliberal theology that weakens urban black political struggles.

and exceed some of these routes to capture without eliminating them altogether. It might even—though such a possibility remains speculative today—nurture energies to exceed capitalism in the future.

Theorists who construe capitalism to be a more closed or generic structure sometimes demean struggles through which new modes of sexuality, religious faith, artistic expression, consumption priorities, renewable energy, and economic collectives are carried across the threshold of legitimacy. To them, the variations across diverse modes of capitalism may appear minor, and every nontotal challenge may even be seen to be a mode of complicity. The options available are now said to be to accelerate the advance of capitalism in the hope it will collapse, to wait for a revolution, to buy in to complicity, or to adopt a style of total cynicism while staying in the game (which amounts to the third option in a different mood).[20] I am not confident such advocates have measured adequately the insufficiency of capitalism to itself, the real value of the pluralizing gains that have been made, or the risks of fascist takeover during periods of high stress.

Karl Polanyi, in *The Great Transformation,* originally published in 1945, glimpsed how capitalism is never sufficient to itself.[21] He

20. For a fine critique of such positions joined to exploration of creative openings in capitalist modes of capture, see Brian Massumi, *The Principle of Unrest: Activist Philosophy in the Expanded Field* (London: Humanities Press, 2017), esp. chapter 2. In chapter 1, however, Massumi may dilute the double processes supported here. Multifaceted democracy moves back and forth across several poles: the forged subject and new processes of subjectivation; representation of subjects and processes by which they form and dissipate; representational pluralism and the agitational politics of pluralization; electoral politics and democratic modes of enactment exceeding them. In multifaceted democracy, each end point subsists in a relation of torsion to the other. You do not, for instance, transcend electoral democracy—that is a route to horror; rather, you generate social movements that periodically bring new identities, ends, or faiths into being. I am uncertain how far the theme of oscillation puts me at odds with Massumi.

21. See *The Great Transformation: The Political and Economic Origins*

was particularly alert to varying types of social ethos that inhabit capitalist societies, attending to Keynesian, fascist, and classical liberal modes. He assumed, however, that the dearth of state market regulations that created the Great Depression—with the ensuing explosion and amplification of fascist movements in numerous countries—would wipe out forever public identification with neoliberal capitalism. No one gets everything right.

Jürgen Habermas later identified, in the early 1970s, the possibility of legitimacy and motivation crises in Western capitalist states. He saw how capitalist priorities of private investment, commodity consumption, the worker as commodity, and technomanagerial drives were partly dependent on lived orientations to the future compatible with them.[22] If the spiritual faith in future capitalist achievement were to wither under the pressure of new experiences, the order could lose tacit support. It would then either face new pressures for transformation or be pressed to extend disciplines already in place to maintain itself. Beliefs in the future could collapse, while the institutions that needed those beliefs continued to plow forward. And indeed, managerial, police, prison, parole, and urban surveillance practices have been extended significantly since *The Legitimation Crisis* was written, crowned by police practices of terror in the United States routinely imposed on young urban African American males.

One thing Habermas did not discern sufficiently is how the privately focused infrastructure of consumption unfolding in several old capitalist societies was making it increasingly expensive for members of the working and middle classes to make ends meet, contributing to their retreat of support for taxes and a welfare

---

of Our Time (Boston: Beacon Press, 1975), where Polyani both seeks to show how economics is embedded in social life and identifies numerous natural and social contingencies that render such theories incomplete to themselves.

22. See Jürgen Habermas, *Legitimation Crisis,* trans. Thomas McCarthy (Boston: Beacon Press, 1975).

state ethos. Perhaps this was partly because he inhabited German capitalism, where state involvement in collective modes of consumption, such as travel, education, health care, unemployment, ecology, and urban culture, were and are far more developed than in U.S. capitalism. Perhaps another reason was a tendency in that text to underplay the partial autonomy of a system of consumption from the specific mode of production with which it is entangled.

Be that as it may, the legitimation and motivation crises Habermas anticipated as possibilities—not certainties—did not unfold. An unexpected event intervened. In the United States, a new alliance between neoliberalism and white evangelicalism was forged in a way that surprised most secular commentators and cut the expected "deficits" off at the pass. This new assemblage, which drew a large portion of white working- and middle-class evangelicals into it, helped to change the shape of American politics, cultural struggle, and economic life for the next forty years. Many of its evangelical participants were later hit hard by the 2008 economic meltdown engendered by the adventures of finance capital, and they have lagged behind several other constituencies in the recovery.

Today, as we have glimpsed in previous chapters, a dispersed white working and lower middle class has become restless again, as it feels itself caught in a squeeze between financial/corporate high rollers who concentrate wealth and income at the very top and a Left that supports pluralism even as it diminishes the importance of working-class grievances. This has encouraged many to support demands to recast neoliberalism in a more explicitly statist direction (it has always been statist in its support of corporate subsidies, its readiness to bankroll a recovery after a banking crisis, etc.); to roll back precarious advances made by gays, blacks, transgender people, Muslims, Hispanics, and other minorities; and to assert American military might in the world even more bluntly. Under the influence of these pressures, neoliberalism and aspirational fascism have edged closer together. The fact that Republicans (as of July 2017) are unwilling to consider impeachment proceedings against Trump after considerable evidence of collusion with a hostile foreign power to shape and invade an American election represents merely one sign of that slide.

In a way that allows us to hear echoes from an earlier period of alliance between German private industrialists and an insurgent Nazi movement, we now face a possibility that may either be transcended or morph into a distinctive brand of American fascism irreducible to its predecessors. It would accelerate institutional racism, immigration bans, deportation drives, misogyny, selective police ruthlessness, the hegemony of one wing of Christianity, and military bravado while practicing a mode of climate denialism that its predecessors never had to ponder. It would allow vigilante violence against vulnerable groups while maintaining a thin veil of deniability about the state's support or tolerance of it. A new fascism would retain competitive party elections while accelerating a host of state and federal practices that discourage poor minorities from getting to the polls as it draws untrammeled and anonymous campaign expenditures from the filthy rich. It is already clear (July 2017), from its composition and early tactics, that the Trump Voter Integrity Commission is really a Trump Voter Purge Commission. Indeed, this fake issue was probably created to draw attention from Trump's refusal to set up a commission to determine how to avoid repetition in 2018 and 2020 of the massive Russian invasion into the American election that did occur in 2016. The regime would collude with foreign powers to manipulate elections and smear its opponents while seeking to plug other "leaks" in the ruling bureaucracy itself. It would retain a privately owned media while cajoling its owners to silence voices critical of the regime and seeking to bury the remaining critical voices under its own Twitter and blog initiatives. It would make even more right-wing court appointments to insulate its violences, intimidations, corruptions, collusions, and surveillances from effective legal action. It would escalate controls over schools and universities already under way. It would give into the standing temptation to mimic the Reichstag event in Germany—when a dramatic event was either engineered or deployed—to vindicate new steps in its drives to mass mobilization and selective intimidation. It would intensify the drive to bring intelligence and police agencies under control, as it increased surveillance and intimidation of critical citizens. It would extend the neoliberal drive to entangle finance and corporate capital with state modes of subsidy, support and collusion. And it would strive to keep its base mobilized through the endless multiplications of Big Lies, distractions, and carefully circulated rumors to keep the defenders of democracy off-balance. The latter would include escalation of the current practice of planting disinformation in blogs to incriminate critical journalists and other critics and drawing *kompromat* more intimately into the nerves of American politics.[23] It would institute a variety of disruptive acts to disable or divert criticisms of these tendencies, led by dangerous military adventures. All that (would) be fascism, American style.

It is uncertain what to do in the volatile circumstances we face, though protests, blog exposés, support of media courage when it occurs, exposés of how the Big Lie Scenario works, active membership in dissident groups, court challenges, attempts to fold more beneficent modes of affective communication into the milieux in which we participate, and intensive electoral organization are all essential.[24] But to focus now on one underlying issue, the current unrest also teaches us (again) that you cannot secure democratic

23. On June 6, 2017, Rachel Maddow reported that she had received an "official" document that showed Trump's collusion with Russia. It turned out upon close examination to be doctored. Had she used it, she could have faced the fate that wrecked the career of Dan Rather in the 2000 election, in which he innocently reported a doctored document about G. W. Bush, later exposed to be false, and was let go by *CBS News*. There is no proof in this case about the source of the doctored document, but it bears close inquiry because implantation of false documents is a tactic of aspirational fascism.

24. In "Toward an Eco-Egalitarian University," in *The Contemporary Condition* (blog), July, 2014, I delineate steps to take to press a university to become a beacon of the sort of practices needed. See http://contemporarycondition.blogspot.com/2014/07/toward-eco-egalitarian

pluralism unless and until its active supporters also become profoundly committed to reducing significantly class inequalities of income, job security, educational opportunity, retirement prospects, wealth, and conditions of work.

A democratic, pluralist Left, treating an egalitarian agenda as seriously as it does the politics of pluralization, will support actively numerous interim projects, proceeding on multiple fronts at the same time to do so. It will seek to recapture a constituency that has been pulling away from pluralism, at least in part because it has been closed out of its advances. It does not suffice to assert that this constituency does not suffer the most. That could have been said about some aspects of life in several other constituencies that have driven pluralizing advances in the past without undermining the importance of those drives. Besides, pundits saying such things should hesitate unless and until they have tasted something of the actual conditions of neglect, insecurity and declining entitlement among the constituencies in question.

What kind of interim projects? Egalitarian pluralists must include and go well beyond sharp increases in the minimum wage. We can, for example, support laws that set upper and lower limits on income and benefits workers and managers of all sorts receive. We can propose competitions between corporations in the same domains, rewarding those that reduce the discrepancy between the highest- and lowest-income workers the most with a tax break and then make such changes mandatory for other corporations in that domain. We can support free tuition in all public universities, as Bernie Sanders did with great success in the 2016 Democratic primaries, letting working-class parents see how their children can now hope to participate in the good life available in this society. We can join those proposals to active support for a stronger class dimension in affirmative action.

-university.html. I agree, of course, that neoliberal forces in the university will fight them tooth and nail. But the effort is worth it, partly for that reason.

We can detail how the established corporate/state-maintained infrastructure of consumption makes it increasingly difficult for blue-collar and middle-class households to make ends meet, as it also discourages them from supporting tax levels to promote the public goods urgently needed in this society. We can then work to recast the shape that public–private infrastructure takes. We can support a single-payer health system, showing how such programs are both more inclusive and less expensive than those now in place. We can set into place legal guarantees so that retirement programs are not curtailed or reduced when a firm faces bankruptcy. We can support massive infrastructure construction in cities and rural areas and make them compatible with an eco-friendly economy.

To foster the possibility of success, such objectives and programs have to be supported with the same intensity by diverse constituencies as those mobilized on behalf of the noble—and precarious—advances in pluralization during the last several decades. Moreover, we need to nurture a host of democratic leaders at numerous sites with charismatic power, leaders who inspire and support generous, horizontal connections rather than either ignoring the role of charisma in politics or pushing that silo spiral of pugnacious authority so dear to fascism.

Of course, the financial media, the Republican Party, many white evangelicals, and Big Donors will cry in shrill voices on the airwaves every day that such programs are far too expensive and socialistic. We must show how such cries always become muted when a Republican big-spending president, such as Reagan, Bush, or Trump, is in office, when he demands massive expenditures for military growth, police budgets, prison construction, territorial walls, devastating wars, tax breaks for the rich, and corporate/financial subsidies of multiple sorts while seeking to cut Social Security and other "entitlements" of poor and low-income people that do not touch the real entitlements of the rich. The very phrase "entitlement programs" is a piece of fraudulence, designed to focus critique on underfunded programs for the poor and declining middle class as it obscures the host of luxurious entitlement programs for the corporate and financial estates.

Moreover, it is not that difficult to devise a progressive tax plan to pay for the needed programs if you cut back on military, prison, surveillance, and fossil extraction subsidies and if you also eliminate tax breaks for second mortgages and the most polluting modes of agribusiness. The key thing is to link new programs and tax changes closely together. Along the way, it won't hurt to publicize how the phrase "national socialism" seriously misrepresents what German fascism actually was. It was fascistic, and it carefully preserved private ownership of the means of production.

The pluralizing Left—a pluralized "we"—can also press hard to reinstate power to a variety of private and public labor unions, opposing stringent state regulations that have been brought against unions even as corporate regulations have been relaxed. It can propose job training programs for areas that have been hit the hardest by deindustrialization and automation, even as it reworks some free trade agreements. The key is to link shifts in subsidies, taxes, market regulations, and state priorities to improvements in the life conditions of working- and middle-class constituencies.

Some Marxists—but surely not all—might contend that such interim changes are impossible in a capitalist order or that we must wait for a communist revolution to occur. But some of these practices are in place in other capitalist regimes today. And numerous attempts so far in the history of capitalism to say definitively what is possible and impossible have been met with surprise, marked in particular by the emergence of fascist-capitalist movements after the Great Depression, the partial success of New Deal social democratic programs in several countries in helping workers and warding off fascist movements, the rise of the New Left and noble pluralizing movements, and the formation of a right-wing evangelical/capitalist resonance machine in America in the early 1980s. The truth is that nobody knows for sure how far such interim programs could succeed in getting widespread working-class support if pressed widely and actively. We don't know for sure, either, just how far the defining axioms of capitalism can be stretched and pulled to promote a more egalitarian, pluralist, eco-friendly world.

Yes, these interim projects will take a lot of heavy lifting, because, again, several institutional tendencies and power loadings of capitalism press against those achievements. But that is not the same as saying that the "logic" of a capitalist structure makes such an interim agenda impossible. Despite what some hubristic analysts say, nobody has established such an implacable logic, as opposed to identifying impressive loadings of power and priority within the variable uncertainties of capitalism. Experimentalism and activism are in order here, not certainty and waiting for the day of revolution.

Capitalism is an inegalitarian regime with several tendencies to ruthlessness tied to an economy of growth oriented to private profit. But it is also never sufficient to itself, and even the current direction of growth can be directed down alternate routes. As has been revealed at key moments in the past, the character and intensity of social movements, the variable quality of the institutional ethos, the surprise of new events, and drives to greater inclusion by a broader range of constituencies, all can make significant differences. That is why fascism was so fateful for German capitalism, the New Deal so important to America, the rise of the evangelical/ capitalist resonance machine fateful for a shift in the priorities of American capitalism, the emergence of Russian cowboy capitalism so critical, and the rise of radical movements in the 1960s and 1970s so influential in spurring a powerful cluster of noble, intersecting pluralizing movements. Today a cluster of cross-regional eco-movements may also be poised at a new tipping point.

One thing for sure, advances on these fronts would not suffice to resolve the long, ugly history of institutional racism with respect to Amerindians and African Americans. But the class composition of such changes could provide some relief for portions of those constituencies, and it might open windows among less hardened elements of the white working class to respond affirmatively to new militant and creative movements on these fronts. In fact, the wide class initiatives and those pointing specifically at indigenous peoples and African Americans must be pursued in tandem, if either is to go far. The latter must include initiatives to protect indigenous lands and to support their current drives to renewable energy; struggles against pernicious state and court efforts to roll back minority voting opportunities; programs to rebuild the urban infrastructure along renewable lines in cities that have been severely damaged by the combination of racism and deindustrialization; massive improvements in urban public education; and much more. It is when strong initiatives to reduce generic class inequality meld with the close entanglements of race and class that a pluralizing, egalitarian culture can make the most advances.

These are also the kinds of changes most apt to curtail periodic support for aspirational fascism in the United States and to broaden constituency support or tolerance—depending on which segments are engaged—for more radical shifts in the public infrastructure of energy production and consumption urgently needed during rapid acceleration of the Anthropocene. Success on the latter fronts, indeed, will both provide more working-class jobs and reduce the flood of refugees waiting in the wings if nothing radical is done on these fronts. The intensification of refugee pressure is one thing that creates happy hunting grounds for aspirational fascism.

Does Donald Trump secretly believe in climate change and welcome fascist pressures that will intensify as droughts, glacier melts, rising oceans, stressed water supplies, power outages, extreme storms, ocean acidification, anti-immigrant sentiment, and refugee pressures grow? I don't know. But it would not surprise me, given his inveterate drive to use Big Lies to support agendas he pursues for other reasons. What some see as a blind tendency to stumble into blunders I see as a kind of aggressive nihilism both organized in some respects and much more primed to stumble in some directions than others. Indeed, Trump's ruthlessness with indigenous peoples—whose legitimate claims to land obstruct his demands to promote fracking projects that endanger water supplies and hasten destructive climate change—reveals again how the conquest of nature and the conquest of vulnerable constituencies are often linked together. The propensities to the conquest of nature and ruthlessness against vulnerable constituencies, again, are fungible traits, as the earlier history of such a crossing from conquering nature to conquering vilified peoples in Nazi Germany showed so well.[25]

So much for a series of possible (though highly difficult) interim changes to support multifaceted democracy and egalitarianism together. If and when such interim changes succeed, large questions will still loom. To respond in a nonrepressive way to the declining role of America in the world and the immense pressures of climate change, it will then be necessary to experiment more actively to advance toward a distinctive type of multifaceted, democratic socialism. Such advances would be inconceivable without success in the interim programs. But, even then, success may be like trying to thread an old regime through the eye of a needle. The best hope to do so is if larger sections of the working and middle classes are drawn into the agenda, as they find some of their heartfelt grievances addressed. That, anyway, is how it seems to me.

Once advances in the interim agenda are made, the privately incorporated growth imperatives endemic to capitalism must then be both tamed and redirected more radically to adjust to a new world. That, again, will encounter extreme resistance. But some measures could start the ball rolling: legally subsidized expansion of worker, housing, consumer, and farm collectives; a host of role adjustments in the domains of work, consumption, church life, teaching, and retirement investments to help nudge the economy

25. For a rich discussion of how the large wetlands on the eastern flank of Nazi Germany were defined in negative ways that paralleled the definitions of "Slavs" and Jews to be removed from that territory so that Germans could colonize it for farms, see David Blackbourn, *The Conquest of Nature: Water, Landscape, and the Making of Modern Germany* (New York: W. W. Norton, 2006), esp. chapter 6, "Race and Reclamation."

elsewhere and to enliven the potential for collective action among the experimenters; consumer movements to reorganize the infrastructure in which households are now constrained to purchase modes of housing, health care, education, culture, energy, food, and transportation that stretch their budgets to the breaking point; a significant expansion of organic farms, free-range livestock, and urban farming; state programs to build and own a renewable power grid; locally initiated movements to rebuild worn-down housing, bikes, refrigerators, stoves, pathways, and old furniture; volunteer efforts to place solar panels on the homes of low-income people to relieve energy costs and support positive responses to the Anthropocene; a renewed focus on local produce, farmer's markets, and slow cooking; and public ownership of energy production, mass transit, and banking.

Such vibrant initiatives—several of which are now simmering in numerous places—could ease consumer budgets and dampen low- and middle-income pressure to support corporate demands for unregulated corporate expansion. This would set the stage for new public support of state and community programs to curtail further corporate autonomy. Together they could point toward a social pluralism with egalitarian promise in which several profit-driven growth demands are redirected and tamed by locally and collectively owned entities. They could also help to generate constituencies eager to make further advances on these fronts. They could point toward a world in which multifaceted socialism is no longer thought to be an oxymoron.

Creative energies on behalf of ecology, plurality, democracy, and egalitarianism could bolster and reenforce one another—that is, if the interim projects are achieved quickly enough to head off the worst recoil effects emanating from the Anthropocene, itself primarily an effect of fossil fuel energy, evangelical denial, plutocratic finance of elections, and neoliberal deregulation.

I certainly do not say that people should be optimistic about the prospects of success. Optimism and pessimism are perhaps not the key questions to focus on today, anyway. The key question today is what kinds of changes might be possible to respond to a historically demanding situation, a situation that harbors tragic possibility.

It is possible—even perhaps probable?—that fascist pressures will intensify under the rocky conditions neoliberals have so actively promoted from 1980 to the present. But such an outcome, with its devastating results, is not now locked into inevitability. We may sit on the razor's edge of time, as Creon did in *Antigone* before he dallied too long to take possible remedial action in response to a crisis he had helped to foment. Today, multifaceted movements of democratic pluralism, egalitarianism, eco-renewal, and capitalist taming are more congruent than opposed, even as there are real tensions between them. One key to success is to draw a larger segment of the working class into those noble pluralizing movements that have inspired so many for several decades.

William E. Connolly is Krieger/Eisenhower Professor at Johns Hopkins, where he teaches political theory. In 2017, the International Studies Association honored him as a Distinguished Scholar in Theory for his work in capitalism, ecology, planetary processes, and pluralism. His recent books include *Capitalism and Christianity, American Style*; *A World of Becoming*; *The Fragility of Things*; and *Facing the Planetary: Entangled Humanism and the Politics of Swarming*.